PRAYER POWER

How *To* *Pray* *When* You Think You Can't

PRAYER POWER

How to Pray When You Think You Can't

Marci Alborghetti

New York, New York

Prayer Power: How to Pray When You Think You Can't

ISBN-13: 978-0-8249-4716-3

Published by Guideposts
16 East 34th Street
New York, New York 10016
www.guidepostsbooks.com

Distributed by Ideals Publications, a Guideposts company
535 Metroplex Drive, Suite 250
Nashville, Tennessee 37211

Guideposts and *Ideals* are registered trademarks of Guideposts.

Acknowledgments

Every attempt has been made to credit the sources of copyrighted material used in this book. If any such acknowledgment has been inadvertently omitted or miscredited, receipt of such information would be appreciated.

All Scripture quotations, unless otherwise noted, are taken from the *New Revised Standard Version Bible.* Copyright © 1989 by the Division of Christian Education of the National Council of the Churches of Christ in the U.S.A. Used by permission. All rights reserved.

Scripture quotations marked (NIV) are taken from *The Holy Bible, New International Version.* Copyright © 1973, 1978, 1984 International Bible Society. Used by permission of Zondervan Bible Publishers.

Scripture quotations marked (NKJV) are taken from *The Holy Bible, New King James Version.* Copyright © 1997, 1990, 1985, 1983 by Thomas Nelson, Inc.

Scripture quotations marked (RSV) are taken from the *Revised Standard Version of the Bible.* Copyright © 1946, 1952, 1971 by Division of Christian Education of the National Council of Churches of Christ in the U.S.A. Used by permission.

Library of Congress Cataloging-in-Publication Data

Alborghetti, Marci.
How to pray when you think you can't / Marci Alborghetti.

Includes bibliographical references.
ISBN 978-0-8249-4716-3
1. Prayer—Christianity. I. Title.
BV210.3.A43 2007
248.3'2—dc22

2006021481

Cover design by Marisa Jackson
Interior design by Gayle Raymer Design
Cover photo by Edward Duarte/JupiterImages
Typeset by Nancy Tardi

Printed and bound in the United States of America

10 9 8 7 6 5 4 3 2

For God.

~

To Charlie.

Table of Contents

Acknowledgments

PRAYER, LIKE WRITING, requires a combination of skill, will and good teachers. God has sent me some great teachers who have also become friends, and I'd like to thank them for making this book possible. Sylvia Savage is the best "pray-er" I know; she lifts me up. Dr. Margaret Crowely, Dr. Marylouise Fennell and Dorothy Strelchun have modeled prayer-in-action for me for most of my adult life, and they're still doing it. My pastor Michel Belt is an inspiration; my Franciscan friend John Ullrich lives in my heart. My long correspondence with Marion Bond West is a constant education! Ellen Adams lives prayer. The *Daily Guideposts* readers who have taken the time to reach out to me by phone or the Internet have shown me the meaning of prayer.

At Guideposts Books, I am grateful for my unflappable editor Andrew Attaway, and for Stephanie Castillo Samoy, whose unstinting kindness and encouragement have cheered me. The support of my family has been vital. And in the tradition of the last shall be first, the words necessary to thank my husband Charles Duffy would fill a book much longer than this one.

PRAYER POWER

How to Pray When You Think You Can't

Introduction

SEVERAL YEARS AGO I was diagnosed with a malignant melanoma, the most serious form of skin cancer. I feel extremely blessed because that cancer and later recurrences were found in the earliest stage and successfully treated. My friend Mary Jane Clark was also blessed in many ways, but not in the early detection of her cancer.

Mary Jane was extraordinarily open about her own battle with her illness. She called me from her home in Colorado after reading a series I'd written about my struggle with cancer. Over the months of her illness, we talked by phone and exchanged many e-mails.

I was not alone in being touched by Mary Jane's courageous and always faithful journey. She stayed in close touch with her large family and her even larger network of friends all over the world. She insisted that we share jokes with her as well as our prayers. Her unwavering faith in the face of painful, intrusive and exhausting treatments was astonishing and inspiring.

One night, after she'd become very ill and had begun to prepare herself for death, she sent a note that was much shorter than her usual messages. She said that she'd become physically incapable of following her customary prayer routine, and she missed it. She was sick, tired and in pain, and her spiritual focus was no longer clear.

When I read Mary Jane's e-mail, a sense of certainty—a grace of understanding—came over me. I knew instantly that she had done all her difficult prayer work, and that now was the time to reap the benefits of her faith. I knew it didn't matter to God whether she was saying prayers or even speaking at all. I knew that God was with her every moment, even if she wasn't as aware of His presence as she'd been in the past. I knew it was time for her to relax into His embrace. Mary Jane died shortly after that e-mail, and I've wondered since whether I'd adequately communicated all this to her. Had I comforted her? Had she understood?

In many ways, this book is the expanded answer I wish I'd given her, the answer I want to give you and the many people who've touched my life with their pain, their hope and their faith. It's a simple answer: We all face obstacles in life; among them are illness, grief, disappointment, failure, anger, fear, addiction, divorce, sorrow and—today especially—a sense of despair about the state of our world. And while any one of these obstacles, or a combination of them, may cause us to feel unable to pray and out of touch with God, God never loses touch with us.

It is my fervent prayer that this book will help you find your path back to prayer and to God, Who, by the way, will be found waiting precisely where we left Him.

Beginning Prayer

I KNOW THAT PRAYER seems difficult for you, if not impossible, right now. This book is meant to help you recover your sense of God, strengthen your faith and rebuild a practice of prayer. But before we begin, let's look at the only formal prayer that Jesus offered us, the prayer He gave to His disciples when they asked Him, "Lord, teach us to pray" (Luke 11:2–4). Every time you pick up this book, you can start here, with the one prayer given us by our Lord. And since it is literally the Lord's prayer, a personal gift from Jesus to each of us, we should offer it back to the Lord as a personal gift, embracing the meaning of each line as it reaches out to gather us into Christ's waiting arms.

Our Father: Lord, help me to remember that You *are* my Father, a caring Parent Who will love and protect me much more than any human parent.

Who art in heaven: Heaven is Your home, Lord, and I thank You for letting me see glimmers of heaven every day here on Earth, in sunrise and sunset, in thunder and lightning and rain-bearing clouds, in the oceans with their rippling waves and tides and the rivers flowing into them, in roses and irises and snowflakes.

Hallowed be Thy name: Father, let me honor Your name in my every word, action, thought.

Thy kingdom come: Let me remember, dear God, that this world is only temporary, that Your glorious kingdom will indeed come. I long to be swept up into it.

Thy will be done, on earth as it is in heaven: Father, in this world, we are often so far from doing Your will as Jesus revealed it. Help me to live my life according to Your will and help make Earth more like heaven.

Give us this day our daily bread: God of abundance, thank You for providing so generously all that I need. Remind me to share what You provide for me so that all may have their daily bread.

And forgive us our trespasses: Without Your continuous forgiveness, Lord, where would I be?

As we forgive those who trespass against us: I should be more forgiving, Lord; show me how.

And lead us not into temptation: Father, I often feel that I'm being tried. Help me to remember that my small trials are nothing compared to those of Your Son, my Brother, and give me the strength and faith to persevere.

But deliver us from evil: Dear God, intervene for me because I am weak, and without Your deliverance I am like a lost and wandering child. Draw me safely into Your protective embrace, Lord.

Amen: You, Father, are the final amen, the way, the truth, the life.

When You're Ill

MARYANN WAS JUST a teenager when she left the farm she'd been raised on in Ireland to board a ship for America nearly eighty years ago. A few years earlier, when she was nine years old, her father had died of pneumonia, a deadly illness that was dreaded in those days as much as cancer or heart disease is today. "He just came home from work and went to bed," she told me in a still slightly surprised voice. "He never got up. Three days later, he was dead."

Her mother had to figure out a way to support Maryann and her two younger brothers. She managed, but it wasn't easy. Maryann smiles as she remembers how her mother always managed to put aside some food or a few coins for "the tinkers" who traveled from village to village hoping to be hired for odd jobs. "We didn't have much," Maryann says, "but my mother always found a way to give them a little something." Still, the opportunities for all three of her children were radically limited by her husband's death. Maryann had two aunts in the States, and they promised her mother they would take care of her. The plan was for Maryann to finish high school, earn money, send it home and then come home herself to marry and raise her own family in Ireland, where she belonged.

"It was hard for her to let me go, but what else was she going to do?" Maryann says. "She knew I'd be coming back, and we needed the money. And my aunts were happy to have me come. America was a big deal then."

In the end it was more than twenty years before Maryann went back, and then it was only for a visit. Like so many young immigrants, she found herself in a country where jobs and prospective mates were plentiful compared with Ireland. She found both, and to her mother's deep disappointment, settled in the land of opportunity. Her life has by no means been easy. She missed her family in Ireland, and now that she can no longer travel, still does. She and her husband never had children, a sorrow she doesn't talk about. She worked hard all her life as a weaver in Connecticut and Rhode Island mills. She was so skilled that she was given the job of weaving parachute material during World War II—a great responsibility, she remembers.

"I always wanted to do a good job on the looms," she says in a thick brogue, "but with that war weaving, I was very worried. We knew what we were making and what it would be used for. That was important. And it was very hard work, much harder than regular weaving because the cloth had to be so strong."

Meanwhile, she cared for her aunts, uncles and cousins through various illnesses. She even built an addition onto her house for one of her aunts when the woman became too ill to care for herself. No sooner did Maryann's husband John, also a millworker, retire, than he was struck with cancer, and the years Maryann had hoped to spend enjoying their retirement were spent nursing him in their home with the help of his two sisters. "He died at home. He never went into a nursing home," she declares proudly from the chair next to the bed crowding the half room that constitutes her world now. When she became ill, no one was around to keep her out of the nursing home. The only family she had left was in Ireland.

What has sustained Maryann during ninety-five years of challenges, backbreaking work, the illness and death of her loved ones, and her own illness? What kept her from panic as a child crowded onto a boat for a journey to a place she'd never seen and couldn't imagine? What enabled her to put aside her fear and board one of the very first transatlantic airline flights to return to Ireland to visit her mother? What moves her to get up and dress herself every day in the half room she pays for with all but a few dollars of her hard-earned Social Security check?

Prayer.

Maryann has prayed all her life. Nothing fancy—in fact, she prefers the rote prayers of her childhood. She doesn't engage in long philosophical dialogues with God, although she feels familiar enough with the Almighty to refer to Him as "the Man Above" and to respectfully question His motives at keeping her here on Earth so long. She credits God with every good thing in her life, small and large, from the fact that her best friend's little dog wasn't injured when he tumbled off her walker while accompanying her on a stroll down the hall, to the strength she was given to care for her husband. "I was never much of a nurse," she recalls wistfully, "but the Man Above got me through that. I took good care of John in those years."

On the other hand, she doesn't hold God accountable for the painful aspects of her life—her childlessness, her husband's relatively early death, the discrimination she experienced in her adopted country, the loneliness and illness of old age or the fact that she lives in a few square feet being cared for by strangers. It would never occur to her to blame God, to do anything but pray.

WHEN WORDS FAIL

Not long ago, almost overnight, Maryann was transformed from a bright, feisty old lady with abundant, carefully styled white hair and neat clothes who made her own bed every morning, read the daily newspaper and prayed constantly, to an invalid who could barely lift her head off the pillow. She had seemed fine during our weekly visit, but as I left she said she felt the sniffles coming on. I didn't think much of it until I returned the next week and was met by a member of the staff. "Maryann's not doing so well," he said quietly before letting me continue down the hall. My heart started drumming when I saw the oxygen sign outside her door.

I walked slowly into the room, stopping short when I saw her. She was in bed; in the two years I'd been visiting her, I'd never seen her in bed, not even when I visited at night. There were tubes in her nose leading to an oxygen tank, and the menacing hiss of the machine filled the room. Her face was gray, her eyes half closed, and her hair lifeless and flat. She was attached to an intravenous drip and catheter, and she had a medicine patch on her chest. I winced, imagining how the patch must tear at her fragile, papery skin whenever it had to be replaced.

How could this have happened? I wanted to shout, as if someone had done something wrong. But there was no one around to blame, and instead, my anguished question made me want to pray.

Although I wanted to pray, I found myself paralyzed. The way I usually prayed was very different from the prayer of the spirited old woman in the bed, much less formal and yet probably much more self-conscious. Should I pray her way or mine? Was I praying to help myself or to comfort her? Could she even hear me? Did that matter? And what was I praying *for*? For her recovery? Would she want to recover if it meant an even more severely limited life?

Should I pray for her to be cured or healed? I had spent a great deal of time trying to define the distinction between the two. A cure, I'd come to understand, meant an end to disease and a return to physical health; healing meant spiritual transformation, a wholeness that was undaunted by the prospect of death. Jesus both cured and healed the many ill people who came to Him. Would He do the same for Maryann? Had I the right to ask for both? Would she want me to, I wondered, remembering how often she asked why "the Man Above" had not yet taken her?

With all these questions careening around my brain, I moved up to the bed, dragging a chair behind me, careful to avoid the wires and tubes tangled all around her. I took her hand, and all my questions ceased. Leaning forward, I laid my head by hers and just started to pray. I said the "Our Father," and the many other formal prayers I knew she loved. I just kept going, remembering prayers and blessings I hadn't said since I was a child. Somewhere along the way I vaguely realized that these words I whispered—words from prayers that I'd classified as "ritual" or "memorized"—were, when I actually paid close attention to them, perfect words of praise. I put that newfound knowledge aside to consider at another time and kept praying.

When I'd finished, wearing out my memory and imagination, Maryann moved her hand a little in mine and said, "All the old prayers. You know all the old prayers."

Yes. The old prayers.

WHAT IS PRAYER?

What is prayer? How do we pray? The answers to these questions need not, indeed *will* not, be universal. Maryann's answer, "all the old prayers," may seem simplistic to those who've made a deep, individualized study of religion and spirituality. But her answer has its own depth and richness, as I came to realize when reciting words full of images of Jesus' life, eloquent praise, pleas for forgiveness and hopeful faith.

Each of us will likely have a different answer to the *what* and the *how* of prayer. Like Maryann's, our answers will depend on our parents, our background, our church community, whether we *have* a church community or other community coming together around a house of worship, our triumphs and our disappointments.

Prayer, at its most basic and vital level, is simply a conversation with God, however we may name God. I Am Who I Am. Jesus. Lord. Brother. *El Señor*. Holy Spirit. Creator. Father. Exalted One. Almighty. The Higher Power. And yes, even the Man Above. In the end, it doesn't really matter by what name we call God, as long as we do, indeed, call Him. And as people who've suffered well know, it is when we are ill, at our weakest and most debilitated, that we most need to cry out to God. It can also be the time when we feel least able to do so.

Those who make prayer part of a daily routine may have a hard time imagining not praying. It's hard to conceive of a situation where we would not choose to pray. But what about a circumstance where there seems to be no choice? When, like Maryann or Mary Jane Clark, we're in too much pain, too weary or too confused by medication to maintain our prayer routine? What happens then?

That's when we return to the basic definition: Prayer is a conversation with God, an ongoing conversation. God is not a demanding conversationalist. He doesn't require us to have a fabulous vocabulary, great learning, a high IQ or deep wit in order to talk to Him. If we are too ill to crawl out of bed, much less go to services or Bible study or fall onto our knees, God will listen to us utter a single word. "Lord." "Help." "Heal." "Please." "Cure." "Father." "Love." "Sorry." "Forgive." "Afraid." "Hurt." "Mercy." "Stay." "Wonderful." "Counselor."

Even those words, surely prayers in and of themselves, needn't be said aloud. A single word or thought, spoken or formed in love, can be more powerful than a long, wordy prayer. So if your mouth is too dry, your tongue too thick, your throat too constricted, the Lord will bend close to you to attend to even a thought, an unspoken prayer. When you welcome God into your heart and mind, you can tell Him about your fear, your pain, your uncertainty, your need for help and forgiveness. Such intimate, silent communication is as sincere a form of prayer as any spoken word. Remember that God does not require our requests to know what we need. He asks only for our love, and the love that reaches out to Him is itself a perfect prayer, without the need for words.

God knows what we need better than we ever could. The hard truth, the truth that almost all of us have a difficult time accepting, especially in times of sickness, is that sometimes the thing we dread the most—suffering, illness, death—is what He has decided is best for us. It is hard to imagine how God could have chosen these things for us, why He would think them best for us. Libraries are filled with books that try to explain this perplexing concept. Theories, from the theological to the ridiculous, have been put forward from the days of Job until today. No doubt more will be offered in the future. Several years ago the name of a brilliant and devout rabbi who had suffered much in his own life appeared for some time on the best-seller list for writing a book called, *When Bad Things Happen to Good People.* Bookstores couldn't keep enough copies on their shelves.

Everyone wants to know the answer, and no one wants to accept the truth, which is that we simply can't know why bad things happen to good people, or why bad things happen at all, for that matter. No one knows! As difficult as it is to accept in these days when some people seem to be concerned with issues of personal power and the struggle for success, we're limited creatures. We just can't fathom the nature of God, nor does it make much sense for us to try. The greatest religious thinkers through the ages have not been able to explain why events unfold in the world the way they do.

Listen to how God finally interrupts and majestically dismisses the confused and sometimes presumptuous musings of Job and his friends about why Job has suffered such calamity.

Then the Lord answered Job out of the whirlwind . . . .
"Where were you when I laid the foundation of
the earth?
Tell me, if you have understanding.
Who determined its measurements—surely you know!
Or who stretched the line upon it? . . .
Have you commanded the morning since your
days began,
and caused the dawn to know its place,
that it might take hold of the skirts of the earth,
and the wicked be shaken out of it? . . .
Have you entered into the springs of the sea,
or walked in the recesses of the deep?
Have the gates of death been revealed to you,
or have you seen the gates of deep darkness? . . .
Where is the way to the dwelling of light,
and where is the place of darkness,
that you may take it to its territory
and that you may discern the paths to its home? . . .
Can you lift up your voice to the clouds,
that a flood of waters may cover you?

Can you send forth lightnings, that they may go
and say to you, 'Here we are'? . . .
Is the wild ox willing to serve you?
Will he spend the night at your crib?"
—JOB 38:1, 4–5, 12–13, 16–17, 19–20, 34–35; 39:9 (RSV)

Yet even with God's magnificent extended answer resounding in our minds, we persist in wanting to know why bad things happen. Is all pain and illness a result of our free will, our bad choices coming back to haunt us? Or is it, as some of the disciples suggested to Jesus when they spotted the blind man in the temple, that suffering is God's way of forcing us to atone for our past sins or even those of our parents? Jesus immediately dismisses this theory, debunking centuries of traditional belief:

And His disciples asked Him, saying, "Rabbi, who sinned, this man or his parents, that he was born blind?" Jesus answered, "Neither this man nor his parents sinned, but that the works of God should be revealed in him. I must work the works of Him who sent Me while it is day; the night is coming when no one can work. As long as I am in the world, I am the light of the world."   —JOHN 9:2–5 (NKJV)

Some people claim that suffering humbles us and encourages us to seek grace and healing, and indeed, these can be the most positive aspects of suffering. Still others say that illness and trouble *force* us to pray; and while it is certainly true that there are those of us who pray only when we are desperate and in need, even the most pious people may find it more difficult, if not impossible, to pray during times of pain. That's where faith comes in.

I have a good friend with whom I often pray. When we pray together, she first offers thanks and praise to the Lord for all that He's doing for us. Then she presents her petitions, both for us and for the world. When she's finished with these prayers, she simply says, "Lord, You are a good God. You are not a God of unfinished business. We leave everything in Your kind care." That's it. And she means it.

ACTIVE PRAYER

I have a friend who's in his eighties; once or twice a month we have a long talk about the challenges we face in living our faith. Now partially blind and plagued by a serious balance problem, he's extremely frank when discussing his difficulties with prayer. "All my life I've believed in the efficacy of prayer," he begins. "I have faith. I pray. I believe in prayer, and I believe that it works. But that's all intellect, all rational thought. Lately, I don't feel it. I don't feel that I'm being heard. I'm not swept away with God's presence when I pray. I don't feel much of anything. It's all very dry."

We talk about making prayer into a conversation with God, and he acknowledges that simply talking with God as with a friend is a wonderful way to pray. But as he tries to become accustomed to a time of illness and "enforced boredom" he still feels little emotion when he prays. He tells me that he felt much better about his prayer life when he was able to maintain an active volunteering schedule. Being with, and doing for, others made a difference. Being active made a difference.

Thinking about his problem has taught me something else about prayer: Prayer is not always a matter of words; prayer, in its purest form, is often action. From the prophets to the apostles, those closest to God proved their devotion more through actions than words. Moses was barely articulate enough to converse with the Pharaoh or even his fellow Hebrews, yet his actions—his *active prayers*—made him worthy of intimacy with the Almighty. Samuel, Jonah, Elijah, Elisha, Peter, Paul, Matthew, John and James did more acting than talking.

Paul traveled all over the known world, often working at his trade of tentmaking to earn his keep in different communities. Was Paul's communal work as a tentmaker any less prayer than his letters and exhortations? He knew that the Gospel was spread as much by example as by preaching. Even eating was an opportunity to share the Gospel with others:

> *I know and am persuaded in the Lord Jesus that nothing is unclean in itself; but it is unclean for anyone who thinks it unclean. If your brother or sister is being*

injured by what you eat, you are no longer walking in
love. Do not let what you eat cause the ruin of one for
whom Christ died. . . . Do not, for the sake of food,
destroy the work of God. . . .   —ROMANS 14:14–15, 20

And when Paul warns the Thessalonians against idleness,
he is urging them to follow his own example and perform
legitimate work as a way of praying and of living the faith:

Now we command you, beloved, in the name of our
Lord Jesus Christ, to keep away from believers who are
living in idleness and not according to the tradition
that they received from us. For you yourselves know
how you ought to imitate us; we were not idle when we
were with you, and we did not eat anyone's bread with-
out paying for it; but with toil and labor we worked
night and day, so that we might not burden any of you.
This was not because we do not have that right, but in
order to give you an example to imitate. For even when
we were with you, we gave you this command: Anyone
unwilling to work should not eat. For we hear that
some of you are living in idleness, mere busybodies, not
doing any work. Now such persons we command and
exhort in the Lord Jesus Christ to do their work quietly
and to earn their own living.   —2 THESSALONIANS 3:6–12

When we're struggling with illness, we would do well to
remember that Paul often referred to his own debilitating

disease—and that Paul did not allow such disabilities to keep him from active prayer.

> *To the present hour we are hungry and thirsty, we are poorly clothed and beaten and homeless, and we grow weary from the work of our own hands. When reviled, we bless; when persecuted, we endure; when slandered, we speak kindly. We have become like the rubbish of the world, the dregs of all things, to this very day.*
>
> —1 CORINTHIANS 4:11–13

Indeed, in his next letter to the Corinthians, Paul even embraces his afflictions because of the positive action that will result from them. Not only does illness bring us the consolation of others, he tells us, but also it brings us the consolation of God:

> *Blessed be the God and Father of our Lord Jesus Christ, the Father of mercies and the God of all consolation, who consoles us in all our affliction, so that we may be able to console those who are in any affliction with the consolation with which we ourselves are consoled by God. For just as the sufferings of Christ are abundant for us, so also our consolation is abundant through Christ. If we are being afflicted, it is for your consolation and salvation; if we are being consoled, it is for your consolation, which you experience when you patiently endure the same sufferings that we are also*

suffering. . . . We do not want you to be unaware, broth-
ers and sisters, of the affliction we experienced in Asia;
for we were so utterly unbearably crushed that we
despaired of life itself. Indeed, we felt that we had
received the sentence of death so that we would rely not
on ourselves but on God who raises the dead.

—2 CORINTHIANS 1:3–9

Even in the midst of illness and affliction, action has been a form of prayer for as long as people have been praying. And it's clear from Scripture that those closest to God are often those who practiced active prayer even when they were sick or debilitated. How can I know if an action or activity is a form of prayer? If it's done with God in my heart and mind; if it's done with a yearning to be close to God or to stay close to Him; if it's done in a conscious effort to serve others as Jesus served us, it is prayer—a hopeful, vital method of communicating with God.

～

My husband Charlie and I recently met a man who embodies active prayer. Twenty-five years ago, Jeremiah Lowney was afflicted with bladder cancer. His doctors gave him six months to live.

An orthodontist with a thriving practice, a wife and four children, Jerry had just begun a long and uncertain road to recovery when he was invited by the Catholic bishop of Norwich, Connecticut, to accompany him to Haiti. The fact-finding trip was part of an effort to encourage wealthier "First World" church members to contribute more to the poorest regions of the world. Jerry's wife Virginia, his aging parents and his doctors were not thrilled about the trip, but Jerry was determined. "I had said I would go to Port-au-Prince," he recalls, "and I was going no matter what." Though he was the only dentist in the group, he didn't expect to do much work, since the purpose of the trip was to explore the problems of Haiti rather than to actually deliver health care. At least that was the plan.

But as things turned out, Jerry, assisted by his son Mark, a premed student who had gone along to monitor his father's health, did little else *but* deliver health care. They performed hundreds of tooth extractions when they weren't learning about the grinding poverty that overwhelms Haiti. On that and subsequent visits over the next few years, Jerry worked mainly in Port-au-Prince at the request of the Missionaries of Charity, the order founded by Mother Teresa. After the initial journey with Mark, Jerry often brought helpers along on his trips, including his other children, his wife and Sister Carla Hopkins, a French-speaking nun who could communicate more easily with the French-speaking Haitians.

Through the Missionaries of Charity, Jerry came to have regular phone conversations with Mother Teresa. In 1985 she told him that she was sending four of her sisters to Jeremie, a city of about fifty thousand located 140 miles southwest of

Port-au-Prince. Mother Teresa told Jerry that the sisters in Jeremie would need his assistance even more than the people in Port-au-Prince. Without hesitation, despite the threats to his own health posed by malaria and dengue fever, he set out for Jeremie. The mountainous region had terrible roads that could be navigated only by an all-terrain vehicle. It took twelve hours to travel the 140 miles. When Jerry arrived, he found Mother Teresa's four sisters setting up a temporary headquarters, and he went to work providing dental care.

A deeply spiritual man whose faith as often as not expresses itself in a dry sense of humor, Jerry observes, "I never got malaria or dengue fever, or even so much as a cold. Of course, my wife and kids got everything!"

When Dr. Julian Joseph, a Haitian anesthesiologist living in Connecticut, and the bishop of Jeremie gave Jerry a parcel of land to set up a clinic, he created the Haitian Dental Foundation and asked Sister Carla if she was willing to remain in Jeremie to oversee the building of the clinic and to serve the residents. Jerry paid for her apartment in town as well as for clearing the land and building the clinic.

Today, the Haitian Health Foundation, a larger and broader version of the original dental foundation, serves more than two hundred thousand people in Jeremie. Jerry and his family run the foundation, traveling to Haiti several times a year. Did he pursue the Haiti ministry as a result of his illness? It's hard to say with Jerry; he certainly didn't let it stop him. He recently talked to me about why he's so committed to active prayer in the form of his Haitian work, even in the face of such devastating poverty and the increasing violence in Haiti.

"You know, since my cancer I've never been afraid of anything in my life. People always talk to me about the horrible state of things in Haiti, the poverty, the illness, the danger. They want to know why we went in the first place and how we avoided becoming discouraged. I can only say that we did things one person at a time. We wanted to bring hope to a hopeless place."

And that was 199,999 souls ago.

HEALING IMAGES

Healing images can also be a powerful prayer for those in the crushing grip of illness, as well as those who feel too confused and troubled to know how to form the right words. Several years ago, I injured my leg and was put on a painkiller. My first hint that there might be a problem should have been the odd feeling that my jaw was becoming unhinged from my face. But I was too dense, not to mention unfamiliar with medication, to see the signs. Besides, my leg felt so much better with the pills!

One day about a month into the treatment, I became so sick that I could barely crawl from my bed to the bathroom and back. I realized I was too weak to even make it down the stairs to the phone. My whole universe was reduced to my bed. I couldn't read or watch television. It hurt just to move.

Although I couldn't sleep, during that night I fell into a state of half consciousness. My mouth and brain seemed incapable of forming prayers; even the simplest words seemed too difficult for me. So I let all that go and thought about Jesus the healer. I saw myself lying motionless, afraid to move lest I aggravate the pain, just as I was in my bed, except that in my mind I was in a garden surrounded by extraordinarily lush flowers, vines and trees. Everything was green, with vivid bursts of color from the blossoms. I knew somehow that the fragrance of the flowers would be over-poweringly sweet, and my stomach started to churn. But then I realized that I couldn't smell the flowers, and imme-diately I understood that God had removed their scent to keep me from being sickened while I rested in this place.

Then Jesus was there. I imagined Him sitting beside me on the warm, dry, bright green grass. Jesus laid His hand on my stomach, and without a bit of pain, my skin opened. The Lord poured warm, cleansing water from a bowl into the opening. It was the same water that would be used to spray and nourish the flowers and plants in the garden. I imagined the healing water coursing through me and the pain and dis-ease being washed away. And for the first time in close to forty hours, I slept. When I woke I was able to go downstairs, call a friend and get to the doctor.

Not all healing imagery need be so detailed. You don't

even have to be ill to make use of healing imagery; in fact, it may be helpful to have some images stored up in your mind in case of future sickness or prayer paralysis.

PRAYING WITH IMAGES

First, put on loose clothing or simply wrap yourself in a favorite quilt or blanket. Go to a place where you are unlikely to be interrupted and sit or lie in a comfortable position. Breathe deeply, close your eyes, relax. Allow your entire body to settle fully into position as if you're planted there and slowly setting down roots. Try to bring some of the following images into your mind, adapting them according to your own experience, your needs, and your own relationship with the Lord.

- Picture yourself lying or sitting in a beautiful, calming setting: for some, this may be a beach; for others, a forest or the top of a mountain; for still others, a church or simply a favorite room. Now see Jesus coming to you here in your very own place, sitting beside you, laying His healing hands on the places that hurt. Recall some of the healings recorded in the New Testament. Think about all the people the Lord has healed and understand that He is here to comfort and heal you as He has all the rest. Imagine yourself part of a vast community of those who have been made well. Allow the healing to flow through you. Allow the presence of the Lord to engulf you. Let yourself feel and appreciate His power. Feel grateful for this gift. Stay there with the Lord for as long as you can.

↪ Imagine God coming for you, coming to heal you wherever you are. Feel the relief of knowing that the Lord is in charge and coming to you. Accept and welcome Him. See Him enter your room or the place where you are with a gentle but purposeful stride. He comes and lifts you into His infinitely strong arms and rocks you like a baby. God rubs your back and cradles your head. Allow the memories you're not even sure you have to come flooding back: memories of what it feels like to be an infant, helpless and dependent. Know that this Parent is a perfect Parent, Who won't disappoint or hurt you in any way. This Parent knows and gives only love. As God holds and comforts you, feel His utter acceptance and love touch every atom of your being. Lay your head on His shoulder, tucked under His chin, and rest.

↪ Build your healing image from the Gospels, using one of the many passages that describe Jesus healing a sick person. For example, if you select the story of the crippled man whom Jesus made to walk (Matthew 9:2–7), you might place yourself in the midst of a crowd gathered to see Jesus. Though you long to just see the Lord, you can't get to Him because you are disabled; certainly you cannot compete with this pressing throng. You feel exhausted, pained and full of despair. You wonder what sins you've committed to be in such a miserable state. Then Jesus stops in the midst of what He is doing with the crowd. He has seen you! Somehow, in this pushy, needy mob, the Lord has seen *you!* He comes over to you, and without your uttering a word, He shows that He knows what you are thinking. You hear Him tell you that your sins are forgiven! Your heart leaps in joy. And then, just so you understand that He has freed your body as well as your heart, He tells you that you are healed.

PRAYER PARTNERING

When prayer is physically difficult, nothing can be as healing and encouraging as knowing that someone is praying with you—or even doing your praying for you. Members of faith communities pray for the sick and the dying at most services. Some congregations have prayer chains and telephone pray-ins that allow prayers for those in need to continue throughout the week. The prayer support and personal contacts available through these connections can be immensely comforting.

During times of illness or disability, prayer partners can be a vital link to a church community and regular prayer routines. Prayer partnering need not be a formal or complicated arrangement. By laying my head on her pillow and murmuring the "old prayers," I became Maryann's prayer partner. When I was emotionally paralyzed by the specter of cancer, many of my friends and readers, some of whom I'd never met or even spoken to, became prayer partners through e-mails, letters and phone calls. Prayer partnering is a simple, loving way to express community and faith in healing. Here are some things you can do to create prayer partnerships:

- ✎ First, make a prayer pact with the most powerful Partner you can ever have—God. This may seem a bit strange. After all, we're praying *to* God, so how can He be a prayer Partner? In fact, God is much more than a Partner in prayer; God is the Guiding Partner in every aspect of our lives, and never more so than when we're sick.

  In her book, *Why Me? Why Now?* breast cancer survivor Lorraine V. Murray writes,

  > If I've learned anything from my cancer diagnosis, it's that the illusion of control over our lives is just that— an illusion. This is not to say we should pull out all the stops, gain one hundred pounds and take up smoking. But it's important to acknowledge that we are not in the driver's seat. Someone Else is steering the big car of life and planning our itinerary, while we are the ones sitting in the backseat. As backseat drivers, we can certainly make our desires known, but we're not ultimately responsible for the outcome of the trip.

So make that your first prayer affirmation. Before you form a prayer partnership with anyone else, acknowledge God's power in your life. Tell Him you know He's in the driver's seat. Embrace His willingness to hear and share your prayers, even when they are not expressed in words, even when they are no more than a yearning toward Him. Surrender to the ultimate prayer Partner, and rejoice in that surrender, for it too is prayer.

- Talk to friends and acquaintances about making a commitment to regularly pray for one another. Meet weekly or monthly, throw your names in a hat and ask everyone to pray daily for the person whose name he or she selects. If a member is ill, becomes ill or requests special prayers, each member will also pray daily for that person. Using the same process, explore the prospect of forging a prayer partnership in your church community.

- Start praying today for someone who is sick or disabled. If possible, let the person know you are praying for her or him. Visit if you can.

- Write a prayer for someone who is sick or disabled. Visit the person and read your prayer aloud. If you can't visit, call and read the prayer to him or her over the phone. Send the person a copy of your prayer so that you can read the prayer together.

✎ Ask a spouse, partner, best friend or relative to become your special prayer partner. Each of you may tell the other what specific prayer needs you have, or you may simply pray for the other's general health and well-being.

✎ You may want to create prayer partnerships before illness comes into the picture; that way, these bonds will already be forged when they are most needed. And remember that prayer partnerships don't have to be limited to people with whom you can have personal, face-to-face contact; you can keep in touch with your prayer partner through letters, e-mails and phone conversations.

THANKSGIVING

Even in the most difficult of circumstances, one of the simplest—and often overlooked—prayers is an offering of thanks. Many of us grew up saying a blessing before meals to thank God for the food, but beyond that, we may not be accustomed to routinely thanking God for the everyday blessings of our lives. Yet this is an important way to communicate with the Lord—and it's also easy! What better way to reestablish our prayer practice than by simply telling God, "Thank You!" for the good things in our lives?

This daily practice also compels us to actually *notice* those small wonders and to constantly remind ourselves that every good thing comes from the Lord. In making these prayers of thanksgiving, remember that this is not the time to make our requests to God—if we wish, we can spend every other hour of the day on those prayers. But when we give thanks, we concentrate on the words that show our appreciation to the Lord.

Although it may be hard at first to think of blessings in the midst of illness, they are there if we seek and acknowledge them. The following prayers are examples of the kinds of thanksgiving you may wish to offer in your illness. Don't be limited by these prayers; adapt them to your own circumstances and put them in your own words. No matter how far from thankful you may be feeling, make thanksgiving a daily practice.

Lord, thank You for my waking this day and the blessings that await me.

Father, thank You for the peaceful sleep I have enjoyed despite my illness.

Merciful Jesus, thank You for the pain-free hour, or minute, I just spent.

Healing God, thank You for the doctors, nurses and medicines that have helped me.

Jesus, thank You for the Gospel stories of Your healing ministry that provide me with hope.

Provident God, thank You for the food I tasted today, and for the nourishment it gave me.

Father, thank You for giving me the courage to try to pray.

Father, thank You for the comfort of my bed and the peace of nighttime.

PSALM-AS-PRAYER

Praying by reading and reciting the psalms can be an extremely helpful and easy way to pray, especially when words of our own are difficult to find. No book of the Bible better expresses the range of emotions, temptations and illnesses we humans are subject to than the Book of Psalms. Many of the psalms are believed to be the works of King David, who as an innocent child, as a young man facing Goliath with unsurpassed courage, as a just and clever rebel warrior and finally as a powerful king, was himself exposed to the full range of human experience, good and bad.

These intensely moving poems or songs tell of victory and defeat, sin and forgiveness, illness and restoration to health, the joy of birth and the grief of death, enmity and reconciliation, pain and healing. Most of all, they speak of the comfort that can be found in surrendering oneself to God. Each chapter in this book will include a psalm selected specifically to address the issues raised in that chapter. However, we should not confine ourselves to a single psalm; every psalm speaks to each individual in a particular way, and exploring these beautiful and profound verses can lead to a deeper and more satisfying prayer life.

PSALM 6: PRAYER FOR RECOVERY
FROM GRAVE ILLNESS

O Lord, do not rebuke me in your anger,
or discipline me in your wrath.
Be gracious to me, O Lord, for I am languishing;
O Lord, heal me, for my bones are shaking with terror.
My soul also is struck with terror,
while you, O Lord—how long?
Turn, O Lord, save my life;
deliver me for the sake of your steadfast love.
For in death there is no remembrance of you;
in Sheol, who can give you praise?
I am weary with my moaning;
every night I flood my bed with tears;
I drench my couch with my weeping.
My eyes waste away because of grief;
they grow weak because of all my foes.
Depart from me, all you workers of evil,
for the Lord has heard the sound of my weeping.
The Lord has heard my supplication;

the Lord accepts my prayer.
All my enemies shall be ashamed and struck with terror;
they shall turn back, and in a moment be put to shame.

SUGGESTED CLOSING PRAYER

Jesus, Lord, I understand that there is a difference between being cured and being healed. When You walked the earth, You performed both healings and cures. I beg that You grant me both, Lord: that my illness be cured and that my spirit be healed. I almost shrink from asking; it seems like so much to pray for. But with You, Lord, all things are possible. I put my faith in You. I ask You also to open me to Your healing power. I know that I am limited by doubt and pain. Allow me to receive Your healing with open arms, an open heart and an open mind. Release me from the fear and hurting that prevent me from turning to You wholly. Let me feel Your healing power move through me, Lord.

BIBLE REFERENCE

And there was a leper who came to him and knelt before him, saying, "Lord, if you choose, you can make me clean." [Jesus] stretched out his hand and touched him, saying, "I do choose. Be made clean!" Immediately his leprosy was cleansed.

—MATTHEW 8:2–3

When You're Facing Emotional Problems

SOME OF THE MOST creative people in history have been vulnerable to mental and emotional illnesses. A long list of artists, writers, performers and philosophers fits the profile. Many of them, including William Styron, Tipper Gore, Vincent van Gogh, Ernest Hemingway, F. Scott Fitzgerald, Marilyn Monroe and Judy Garland, have either acknowledged their struggles publicly or lost their lives to them. And many people of deep faith have suffered from periods of sorrow, despair, fear and anxiety.

Perhaps life is revealed sharply to those who live with emotional illness in a way that makes them more vulnerable to extreme joy, sorrow, anxiety and pain. They find it hard or impossible to screen out the difficult aspects of life, the things that can paralyze us or keep us stuck in an unstable or even dangerous life pattern. Perhaps we all feel this way at one time or another; I know I've often felt unprotected from the bombardment of life's staggering realities. My experiences with the people I meet through my writing and in a support group I run for those living with depression and anxiety suggest that the number of people confronting such mental distress is only growing in our complex and often frightening world.

Mental and emotional illness is often a function of a person's physical and biological makeup. Hereditary factors play an important role. Increasingly, doctors are successfully treating emotional illness with a combination of drugs to address the biological aspect of the problem and counseling to sort out the emotional issues. In some cases drugs alone can reverse or at least blunt the course of the disease.

These are all positive developments that reduce the stigma too often attached to mental and emotional illness. Not long ago people who were victims of such disturbances were often viewed with the kind of suspicion and even disdain that would never be directed toward people with heart disease or cancer. The "news" that mental illness is often a result of chemical imbalances has helped to free its victims from embarrassment and shame.

The way we respond to emotional distress depends in large part on our individual biology. Many of the people I've talked with have had severe anxiety attacks, which closely mimic heart attacks and can include shortness of breath, pain in the arms, blurred vision, nausea and an inexplicable and abrupt terror of one's surroundings. More crippling than the attacks themselves can be the fear they cause in their victims. After undergoing an anxiety attack, many people are afraid to leave the house. Others display obsessive-compulsive behavior that can include constant hand washing, repetitive movements and the compulsion to repeat the same number or phrase over and over again. In some cases people experience wide mood swings, feeling crazily happy and unnaturally energetic for a period, and then suddenly miserable and depressed.

Addiction is often associated with mental and emotional illness, and whether an addiction is a symptom of some underlying problem or actually the disease itself is probably not important. What is important is that any active addiction can severely diminish, if not destroy, the ability to pray. But as we see with the success of groups like Alcoholics Anonymous and similar Twelve-Step programs, addicts are deeply in need of prayer—their own and those of others. These organizations encourage their members to practice the ultimate form of prayer: acknowledging personal weakness and surrendering to God. This is vital for any successful prayer program, indeed, for any successful life. Addiction, like other mental illnesses, deceptively allows the victim to believe that he or she is in control, and this kind of false confidence or misguided power nudges us away from God. Recognizing and embracing our limits and God's power is the first step to prayer; in fact, for those of us suffering from mental illness, acknowledgment is a prayer.

No matter what we name our maladies, all of us to some

degree or another experience emotional or mental distress. I've come to believe that those who don't feel some level of anxiety, depression or anger about difficult events in their lives are either the saints who have achieved communion with God or people who simply don't care about life. Most of us, however, will have to deal with emotional distress at some point in our lives.

Regardless of the cause, mental and emotional illness have a negative impact on your prayer life. Any significant emotional distress can make it difficult, if not impossible, to keep a regular prayer routine. More serious mental illnesses will make it hard to attend services or regular church community meetings. Fatigue and an inability to focus can sometimes result from necessary medications, while the exhaustion that accompanies depression and some mood imbalances is a serious obstacle to prayer. You may feel ashamed of your difficulties and how they manifest themselves in your life. You may also have feelings of unworthiness, thinking that you've somehow separated yourself from God because of your emotional unrest. All of us confront these same impediments to prayer to some degree at some point in our lives.

At times of mental or emotional distress, the first order of prayer is to *reject* self-defeating thoughts and statements and to create the open space you need to *accept* God's love. You may not be accustomed to thinking of prayer as an emptying of your self-abusive thoughts, but this first essential step allows you to recognize and welcome God, Who is with you and within you. It's a way to fight for your divinely given status as a child of God, Who wants you to enjoy the pleasure and peace of His presence.

Begin to practice making room for God by consciously driving out crippling and poisonous thoughts like the following:

"If God loved me, I wouldn't feel this way, I wouldn't be this way."

"I'm not worth the effort my family and friends make to help me. No wonder some people have given up on me."

"I'm not worth God's time."

"I'm too tired to welcome Jesus into my life."

"With all the huge troubles in this world, God certainly doesn't have time for my pathetic problems and worries."

"If I can't even get to church or recite the prayers I learned as a child, what's the point of trying to pray at all?"

"I'm so disgusted with myself, I know that Jesus cannot love me!"

All these thoughts are wrong! Jesus loves you, and in His life on Earth, He paid particular attention to those devastated by emotional illness. Passage after passage in the Gospels shows Jesus healing people's spirits and driving out

cruel illnesses. In Matthew 8:28–34, we see that even violence does not deter Jesus from healing two dangerously ill
men in the country of the Gadarenes. In Matthew 17:14–18,
Jesus is frustrated at the lack of belief among the crowd just
before He cures a boy who has horrible fits.

In Mark 1:23–26, Jesus encounters a man with an
unclean spirit in the Capernaum synagogue; recognizing the
man's faith, Jesus heals him on the spot. In Mark 7:25–30,
Jesus steps across the boundaries of race, religion and
nationality to heal a troubled daughter of a Syrophoenician
woman. Perhaps the most heartening of Jesus' many healings
of those trapped by mental illness is His compassion for
Mary Magdalene, the woman who was to become one of the
most faithful disciples.

You can take any of these healings as your model and
your source of hope. Just as the Lord saw the suffering of the
people He lived among two thousand years ago, so He sees
your suffering now. Take courage in knowing that He hears
your prayers, no matter how you pray: with words, without
words, in church, in your room, by emptying yourself of
negativity, by filling yourself with Scripture. There is no
right or wrong way to pray as long as you yearn for the presence of the Lord and open your heart to Him.

Now that you have prayerfully driven out the negative
thoughts that are obstacles to your lifelong conversation
with God, you can begin to fill that newly cleansed space

with positive prayer statements. These can include the following affirmations:

"God loves me. I am His own child. I am special to God."

"I welcome the gifts that come with my burden:

- *⬧ the gift to see things in a different way than others, just as the prophets and disciples did;*

- *⬧ the gift to constantly acknowledge my weaknesses before God and rely on His strength;*

- *⬧ the gift of compassion toward others as a result of my own suffering; and*

- *⬧ the gift of living in a time when medicine and therapies are advanced enough to offer me both relief and hope."*

"Those who have turned away from me are struggling with their own problems. Their reaction is no real reflection on me, and I can pray for them. I do pray for them."

"Those who love and support me do so because they see the value in me. I am grateful to them and to God for bringing them to me."

"I can pray right where I am just with my thoughts and my hopes. I don't need to go somewhere specific to pray. God is with me now."

"I welcome Jesus just as I am, just where I am, as tired as I am, as sad as I am, as ill as I feel. I welcome Him by simply opening my heart and knowing that I need not wait, for He is already present."

"It is when I am most disappointed in myself, when I feel weakest, that the Spirit of God is with me in the strongest possible way."

IMAGING GOD

Earlier I observed that highly creative people may find themselves subject to the sorrows of emotional unrest because they are more vividly conscious of the troubles and anguish in their own lives and in the world. Someone once told me that "creative people don't have strong enough screens to sift out the bad stuff in life." I was struck by this very clear image, and it started me thinking of how we are just a little like God in this. Surely, the Creator does not screen out the suffering of His Creation. If we hurt because we are merely conscious of these things, surely the Father feels deeply when He sees the state of His children and the world He gave us. What better evidence is there than Jesus that God understands our suffering? We cannot begin to imagine how much Jesus shouldered on our behalf.

Identifying with God this way can help you to pray. You can use your sharpened awareness to envision the God Who suffers with you, loves you and listens for your voice.

After emptying your mind of negative and self-defeating thoughts, welcome God into the space you've created. Quiet your mind as much as you can. Don't be concerned if you can't reach a state of total calm or mental silence: as we've seen, God well understands the "noise" that assaults us, and a sincere effort is more important than complete success.

When you've done the best you can to create a quiet space in your mind and spirit, allow an image of God as the loving, empathetic Creator to enter your mind's eye. If a traditional image that you've taken from childhood comes to mind and is pleasing to you, use that image. If you have a favorite painting of Jesus, use it. Again, don't worry if the image that comes to you is different from traditional depictions. If you prefer to imagine God's presence in a warming beam of light, a vast and many-hued ocean, a chilly and starlit night, a nurturing rain or a majestic mountain, allow that image to fill your empty space.

Whatever image comes to you, spend some time with it. Observe it closely. If it is an image of Jesus healing Mary Magdalene, allow the scene to develop in your mind. See Jesus sit on the ground where Mary lies, her eyes wild and glazed, her clothes wrinkled and stained. Watch Jesus place His strong, callused hands on her grimacing face. See her stop writhing as her limbs straighten and she slowly manages to sit up. Observe her facial muscles relax and her eyes clear into a look of surprise, comprehension and, finally, amazed joy. Watch as her fists unclench and she covers Jesus' hands with her own as if to feel what He feels in healing her. See her skin become clear and glowing. Allow yourself to feel this healing in your heart. See and feel what is possible with the Lord.

If you bring another image into your mind, allow it to fully develop in the same way. If you've welcomed God's presence in a warming beam of light, lie down to rest in that splash of light. Feel the warmth. Discern the various colors of the spectrum. See how the sunlight brings life to the earth and all around it. Watch the most magnificent floral blooms rise up before your eyes to drink in the light. Observe how the many creatures of the earth are drawn to bask in the light. Rejoice that you, like them, are welcomed into the Lord's presence.

If your image is of the ocean, feel the water on your skin, bathing you with a bracing chill or warming you to drowsiness. Taste the salt on your tongue. Note the many vibrant and subtle shades and colors of the sea, reflecting the skies and clouds and showing the ocean floor. Observe the creatures who live and move and hunt and flourish in the ocean, from the tiniest algae to the big fish that would make Jonah's appear small. See how they move fluidly and naturally through the depths, leaving no trace once they are gone. Feel the embrace of their Creator in the swell of a cresting wave.

If you seek God in a starlit night, feel the cold air on your skin, calling your every cell to shivering attention and new life. Try to count the stars until you surrender joyfully to a magnitude beyond your knowledge. Be aware of the creatures who live in the night, moths and owls, raccoons and hedgehogs. Watch them move securely through the dark, their own habitat, with the certainty born of knowing they belong to God. Join them in that certainty, that blessed security.

If God visits you in a nurturing rain, look up and feel the drops on your face, cleansing and purifying you. Let the rain run into your eyes so that you may weep God's tears at such munificence. See the rain transform the earth as the parched dirt drinks greedily and the straw turns to soft, green grass. Note how the colors of the world are softened and made kinder under the canopy of clouds and in the refraction of the raindrops. Watch the rainbow form in all its magnificent glory and realize that its rays flow from your heart and end in God's hand.

If the presence of God rises before you as a majestic mountain, allow yourself to marvel at its size and power. See the snow on the peak, the lush grass and the profusion of wildflowers on its slopes, the prosperous villages and fertile farms at its base and cradled in its valleys. Try to guess the time of day by the play between the sun and shadows on the mountainside. See the wild goats roaming the heights. Hear the trickle and then the roar of the streams that flow down from the snowmelt, feeding the land below and forming rivers that wind for miles. And remember that at the Lord's command, even such a mountain can be moved as though it were a hill of sand and hurled into the sea.

If you have trouble bringing a complete image into your mind, start with a simpler practice. Allow a positive word that you associate with the Lord to come into your thoughts: *Father. Parent. Beloved. Friend. Supporter. Healer. Creator. Protector.* Concentrate on just this word. If an image comes to mind, fine; if not, simply keep the word in your mind. Let it rest in the space you've emptied for the Lord. See the letters. Think about what that word means to you and why you associate it with God. Let your thoughts form around the word. Allow a sense of peace and healing to flow from it. This is God with you. This is prayer.

Using Symbols

When emotional distress makes concentration on spoken or written prayers difficult, you can use symbols to keep your heart and mind in a place of prayer. My home is filled with symbols that remind me of how deeply God has manifested Himself in my life and that strengthen my faith in His presence. They help me to make prayer a part of every corner of my life.

You probably have symbols and representations in your home that can lead you to prayer if you recognize and welcome the opportunity they give you. Here are some I use to prompt me to prayer.

- I leave my Christmas manger up year-round, because every time I look at it, I'm both awed and comforted by the hope that it provides a visual symbol of God's extraordinary love for us. The sight of the figures never fails to give me a shimmer of the joy and anticipation that lives in our hearts every Christmas season, and moves me to pray, "Lord, I am comforted that You chose to come to this difficult, confusing, ailing and often cruel place called Earth. I am inspired and thrilled by Your birth."

Even if you don't usually put up a manger at Christmastime, you might consider placing one in easy sight, where you can see it during this time of distress.

SHORT PRAYERS

↝ Crosses hang in every room of my house: from my computer, from pictures of friends and family, from photos of my husband and me, from my jewelry holder. Whenever my husband Charlie travels, I slip a small cross in a rosewood box into his luggage. All of our crosses remind me of what Jesus gave for us, and those I've placed in various spots have specific meaning for me: The cross on my computer is a prayer for guidance in my work; the crosses on pictures of friends and those I love are prayers for their health and salvation; the crosses with my jewelry are reminders that I can carry a representation with me always; the cross that accompanies Charlie in all his travels keeps him close to Jesus and keeps us close together even when we have to say our prayers over the phone. In the cross, we have the ultimate representation of how much God loved us, how much He was willing to endure and suffer to save us.

When I see a cross, I pray, *"Jesus, guide my life and my work. Words cannot express what I owe You; help me to express this debt in how I live, love, work. Protect and save the ones I love. Let those who are far away know that I care for them. Let those who are close see my love in my words and actions. Let my love be but a tiny reflection of Yours."*

✧ As a child I was always so excited to receive the palm fronds given out in some churches on Palm Sunday to mark the triumphant entry of Jesus into Jerusalem. Now I take the palms home and put them in the pots with my indoor plants so that all year long I can see the symbol of Jesus' triumph and courage amid the leaves and flowers of my indoor garden. Whenever I see the palms I'm reminded of how the road Jesus took led to His death and Resurrection—and to our salvation.

My palm fronds move me to pray, *"Lord, how excited You must have been to enter Jerusalem in triumph, and how hurt You must have been when the same people who wildly cheered You rejected You just a few days later. These palms remind me that You relied only on the Father's constant love, and not on the fleeting affections of us humans. Sometimes I feel surrounded by words and people I cannot understand. Help me to stay calm and focused on You."*

ᵔᵔ A metal sculpture depicting the Last Supper hangs on the wall of my kitchen symbolizing the Lord's presence with us and His blessing on our meals and housework. In the midst of those He loved the most, Jesus established the Holy Supper for them and for us.

As I stand in my kitchen, I pray, *"Jesus, be with me now and please bless our food and all in this kitchen that helps me to prepare meals and keep my home orderly. Let me feel Your spirit, Your support, Your peace as I cook, clean and eat. Like Your companions in the Upper Room, let me be nourished and healed by Your presence."*

ᵔᵔ Angels of all shapes and sizes abound in my house: hanging over my exercise bike, floating on my bookcase, rejoicing over the manger, attached to a telephone jack, lined up on the windowsills. They urge me to prayer by reminding me of the role angels play throughout God's creation. The crystal angel over my bike glimmers in the sunlight and reminds me that exercise, even when most tiring, can be offered to the Lord. Those on my bookcase teach me to look for spirituality in my reading. The ones dancing by the manger remind me of the joy they felt at the Lord's birth, the culmination of all they'd worked and waited for. The telephone-jack angel tells me to be kind in my communications, and those on the windowsill remind me of the beauty outside my home and spreading throughout creation.

When I look at my angels, I pray, *"Father, thank You*

for sending angels to touch every part of my life, even as they touched every part of Your unfolding creation. As Jacob and Abraham and so many others of Your faithful followers wrestled with and learned from angels, let me wrestle with and learn from the angels You send me. And let my faith be as simple and complete as that of the angels."

❖ Candle stubs are scattered in various places in my house: in a basket full of cards, prayers and correspondence; among petals of dried flowers I've saved from bouquets Charlie has given me; leaning against a corner on a window. The candles come from Easter services I've attended over the years, and to me they are a testament to the power of Jesus' Resurrection. They remind me of new life, hope, victory, salvation. They tell the story of the wordless prayer of the empty tomb, where the birds happily greet the perfect dawn.

My Easter candles move me to pray: *"Risen Jesus, let the flame of hope You send me bring light, clarity and joy to my life every day and night. Hallelujah!"*

USING REPETITION

I have a tendency to behave compulsively when I feel stress. I went to see a counselor friend because I was worried about responding to anxiety with repetitive actions instead of prayer or calm faith. The behavior was relatively mild, but I wanted to know if I was offending God by these seemingly petty and silly actions.

My friend told me the story of a classmate of his who suffered from obsessive-compulsive disorder. This young man felt the need to repeat certain prayers or phrases—particularly the name of Jesus—a given number of times every day. At first it seemed to everyone that he had a real problem: How would he concentrate on his studies? How would he deal with life after school? But then the people around him discovered that his daily recitals were not a source of shame or anxiety for him. Indeed, he saw them as a legitimate way to pray, because he formed these prayers with a loving, worshipful intent.

"How could anyone argue with that?" recalled my friend. "What could be a more sincere recognition of God in a person's life than to repeat His name silently throughout the day? My classmate had learned to use his disability as an aid to prayer rather than an obstacle to it. Who could honestly claim that God did not love such a constant, faithful expression of weakness?"

I welcomed this modern parable, at first because it seemed to let me off the hook, and later because there appeared to be a real lesson in the life of that young man. God welcomes us no matter how flawed and weak we may be at the time we come to Him, no questions asked. We don't have to get healthy to go to God; God *makes* us healthy.

If your heart is sincere and your spirit is yearning for God, don't worry if you're unable to make long or flawless prayers. If you can't stand up and give testimony, God doesn't care. When you feel oppressed or stuck in your weakness,

God is still strong enough. Simply by calling on His name or repeating a favorite prayer phrase silently or out loud, we make music for the loving ears of God, no matter how discordant it may sound or seem to others.

CENTERING PRAYER

If people living with mental and emotional distress could pray for just one thing, it would most likely be peace. When I'm in the throes of my own deep feelings of anxiety or sorrow, I crave tranquility, deliverance from the chaos that crowds in on me. I once told my pastor that I felt selfish when I took the time and did the things necessary to achieve quiet and calm in my life. I felt guilty when friends and family accused me of acting "like a hermit." They felt rejected. My pastor reminded me of how often Jesus walked away from "the maddening crowd" in order to be alone, regain His strength or simply commune with His Father.

"And it wasn't just the crowd that Jesus left behind," my pastor observed. "As often as not, He would walk away—hide, even—from His disciples and family. When He needed a break, He took it. And that probably helped Him to be a better teacher, a better friend, a better man. Do you think you can be better than Jesus?"

I've remembered my pastor's counsel as I've reread about Jesus secluding Himself in order to rest or pray in peace: "Immediately he made the disciples get into the boat and go on ahead to the other side, while he dismissed the crowds. And after he had dismissed the crowds, he went up the mountain by himself to pray. When evening came, he was there alone" (Matthew 14:22–23). I take comfort in knowing that our Lord, too, needed periods of uninterrupted calm in His life.

However, like Jesus, we are never truly alone. When Jesus went away to pray, His Father was with Him, in Him. This Oneness is what Jesus sought in these solitary hours. By taking time to be alone, you can create prayer with your silence and seclusion by reaching out to God. To the extent that it is possible, seek to be one with God. Obviously, none of us are divine as Jesus is, but as men and women we are created in God's image and likeness, and as believers, we have the promise that God dwells within us. Centering Prayer is a way to seek and celebrate that divine presence. And it is a particularly useful practice for people experiencing mental or emotional distress because the calming effects of a forty-five-minute session can last for an entire day or longer. The mind and body are usually more at peace and able to cope with the events of the day.

Dan, the church leader who taught me Centering Prayer, was a lean, athletic, older man with a short military-style haircut who clearly took good care of himself both physically and spiritually. His practice of Centering Prayer was an integral part of his commitment to physical, emotional and spiritual health. During the very first class, Dan assured those of us who worried that our anxiety and mental unrest might get in the way and that perfect concentration, absolute stillness and a completely relaxed body were not necessary for practicing this prayer-meditation.

Then Dan told us the story of one of the men who'd devised and first taught Centering Prayer. This man often had to travel and tried to practice Centering Prayer once a day even when on a trip. One morning he found himself with an hour or two before his flight, and so he settled down in his airport hotel room for a Centering Prayer session.

"I had a difficult time getting my mind to a place of peace because I'd just finished a conference," he later told Dan. "I was still thinking about the past few days. When I finally did get quiet, a series of huge jets began taking off, one right after another. The hotel just about shook! I stuck with my prayer, but when the time was over I was sure I'd achieved nothing. I told myself it had probably been a waste of time, and my only comfort was that I'd stayed with my routine. Do you know that I had one of my best days after that session! It was as if I'd had the most relaxing, fruitful half hour of Centering Prayer of my life! That really taught me a lesson: God can touch us in spite of ourselves and our circumstances."

Dan went on to tell us that people might experience the practice differently. "My wife," he said with a smile, "often falls asleep. And that's okay if it happens once in a while. In fact, when it happens, it's probably supposed to happen." For most of us in the class, the thought of taking a short nap in the presence of God was like, well, heaven! Relaxation and sleep did not come easily to most of us, and the idea of a prayer that would get us in touch with the Divine while also letting us sleep was astonishing. An hour later, after we'd prayed, most of us were feeling calm and relaxed in ways we'd not experienced in a long time.

Here's a form of Centering Prayer I've found particularly helpful:

First, remind yourself not to demand too much of yourself; this practice is meant to help you "relax into the arms of God." Then get comfortable. Sit comfortably in a chair or sofa or on the floor, or lie down—though your chance of falling asleep is slightly greater in this position!

Breathe as evenly as possible, inhaling from the center of your body, below your chest. When you inhale, let your stomach expand with the breath; when you exhale, let your stomach contract with the breath leaving you. Focus on this as you do it, because many of us don't pay much attention to how we breathe.

Start to consciously relax. Spend as much time as you need to in order to relax each region as fully as possible. Begin with your toes: let all the tension flow out of the tips of your toes and wiggle them; feel them become heavy as they rest. Then go to your ankles: let all the pressure and pain flow out of the pores of your skin and move your ankles in a circle before letting them grow heavy as they rest.

Proceed up to your knees and thighs, continuing to breathe fully and deeply as before. Relax your knees, legs, pelvic region, spine and stomach. Picture each part of you relaxing and resting in the Lord.

Relax your neck and head, letting each part of you grow heavy as it rests. Let the stress you've been carrying around in your brain flow out of the top of your head.

Now imagine a fountain flowing out of your heart. It is filled with pure, clean water like that from the well where Jesus met and cleansed the Samaritan woman. Imagine that water flowing through you, washing away your tensions, your restlessness, your maladies, your pain. Let the purifying water, once it has done its work, flow out of each and every one of your pores.

Now listen to the silence. Listen to your breathing in the silence. Your whole body should feel heavy, weighing deeply on the chair, couch or floor where you are settled.

As you breathe in, silently say the first syllable of a word, or the first word in a two- or three-word phrase. Each time you exhale, finish the word or phrase, drawing it out to match the breath leaving you. This word or words should have a calm, hopeful meaning for you. Many people use the name of Jesus; some say something like *Help me*, inhaling on *Help* and exhaling on *me*.

Select the word or words that most appeal to you. They needn't be the same every time you practice Centering Prayer, although you are certainly free to stick with whatever word works well for you. Your word or words should recognize the presence of God within you, the presence you are now embracing.

Continue silently repeating your word or phrase for at least half an hour (you may want to set an alarm or timer in case you fall asleep). When you feel you've finished, slowly bring your thoughts back to where you are, asking God to stay present in you and with you. Allow your body to become reenergized with His power. Remind yourself again that you are calm and that God is with you. When you are ready, get up and go about your day, remaining conscious of God working in, through and with you.

Praying for Others

One of the best things I can do when I'm ill or debilitated is to focus on others. So when mental or emotional difficulties are making it hard for you to pray for yourself, try to keep on the path to God by praying for others.

Start by asking God to help you to turn your eyes outward, away from your own concerns and problems, for just a few moments. Then focus first on the people who are helping you—family members, friends, doctors, therapists, counselors, the members of your support or therapy groups. You're already connected to these people, and if you think carefully, you may already have an idea of the ways in which they need your prayers. Identify one particular person you'd like to pray for. Think about the person in light of what you have learned in your interactions with him or her. Try to think of something about the person that might need your prayers.

Did your pastor seem distracted during your last counseling session? Could he be worried about church finances or other administrative issues? Pray for his peace of mind, faith and practical solutions to church dilemmas. Was your sister unable to spend much time on the phone during your last call because her child was having problems? Pray for her to have the patience and strength to deal with all her family challenges. Pray that her spouse and her children will work with her to build a stronger family. Did your doctor look tired and pale, or seem impatient? Think about how difficult it must be to hear about the sorrows, pains and troubles of others every day, and pray for his health and easy rest. Was your psychiatrist running late and seeming a bit harried in your last consultation? She might be overextended in her professional obligations, so pray that she'll reconsider her priorities and find time for herself.

The important thing in this kind of prayer is sincerity. It's hard to stop thinking about your own pain long enough to focus on what others might be going through, but it's worth the effort. Truly devoting your thoughts and prayers to the needs of another is a blessed thing, and a wonderful way to pray.

And once you've embraced the idea, there's no limit to this kind of prayer. Does someone in your life need prayers for his or her family? Did you overhear the doctor's receptionist having a furious whispered conversation with her husband? Pray for the strengthening of their marriage. Did a co-worker share his discouragement over a parent with advancing Alzheimer's disease? Pray for the parent and the child, using your own sorrow and pain as a point of empathy.

When you've truly mastered praying for others, you can pray for those you've never met. The researcher who developed the medication you use needs your prayers as much as the good friend who takes time for you every day. Pray for him or her to have a clear mind and a positive work environment. Pray that she loves her work. Pray that she'll be able to develop another drug that will help countless others. Pray for the parents or mentors that made it possible for her to receive her education. Pray for all her teachers, from those who encouraged her as a child to those who taught her in college. Pray for those along the way who supported her in her journey. Pray for her own health. Pray for her husband and children, not only that they thrive and flourish, but also that they appreciate her work and her contributions. Pray for her safety as she travels back and forth to work. Pray that her life outside of work is fulfilling and blessed.

When you make this kind of prayer a way of life, you can focus on a new person every day. This needn't be a prolonged exercise. When time is short, simply hold the person in your heart as you move through your day.

THANKSGIVING

These prayers of appreciation are particularly suited to people living with mental or emotional unrest. Feel free to experiment and use your own experiences when giving thanks.

Father, thank You for the patience and support shown me by the person or people in my life who understand what I'm going through.

Jesus, my Brother, thank You for healing Mary Magdalene, that troubled child from another nation, and so many others. Thank You for Your compassion for all the many kinds of people whose lives can be torn apart by mental distress.

Almighty God, thank You for the moments of peace I enjoyed this hour, this day.

Comforter, Spirit of healing, thank You for the therapists, counselors, ministers and medications that help me.

Lord, thank You for the books and music and even the television programs that soothe, entertain and divert me from my distress.

Dearest Jesus, thank You for helping me to pray for others, to concentrate on lives outside of my own.

PSALM-AS-PRAYER

This prayer for help eloquently reflects the anguish of someone experiencing mental or emotional distress. Food *does*
taste like ashes. The loneliness *does* seem to be that of a wild,
solitary little owl who has no protection, no friend. Bones
and skin *do* ache and wither. We can feel—however falsely—
that God has turned away from us. And just as the psalm
precisely describes these agonies, it offers hope in its awareness of God's constant presence.

PSALM 102:1–11, 18–22
A PRAYER TO THE ETERNAL KING FOR HELP

Hear my prayer, O Lord;
let my cry come to you.
Do not hide your face from me
in the day of my distress.
Incline your ear to me;
answer me speedily in the day when I call
For my days pass away like smoke,
and my bones burn like a furnace.
My heart is stricken and withered like grass;
I am too wasted to eat my bread.
Because of my loud groaning
my bones cling to my skin.
I am like an owl of the wilderness,
like a little owl of the waste places.

I lie awake;
I am like a lonely bird on the housetop.
All day long my enemies taunt me;
those who deride me use my name for a curse.
For I eat ashes like bread,
and mingle tears with my drink, because of your indignation
and anger;
for you have lifted me up and thrown me aside.
My days are like an evening shadow;
I wither away like grass.

. . .

Let this be recorded for a generation to come,
so that a people yet unborn may praise the Lord;
that he looked down from his holy height,
from heaven, the Lord looked at the earth,
to hear the groans of the prisoners,
to set free those who were doomed to die;
so that the name of the Lord may be declared in Zion,
and his praise in Jerusalem,
when peoples gather together,
and kingdoms, to worship the Lord.

SUGGESTED CLOSING PRAYER

All-knowing Father, You are keenly aware of my struggles. You made me, Lord! You know my sorrow, my fear, my shame. You know how deeply I want to believe, to stay focused on Your love and Your glory. Help me, Lord. Keep me centered on You. Fill my eyes and my mind with positive, healing images. Send me the people who will support me in my quest for physical, emotional and spiritual wholeness, and open my eyes so that I may recognize and reach out to them. Steady me in my journey, Lord. I know You are here with me; let me feel Your presence.

BIBLE REFERENCE

He entered the synagogue and taught. They were astounded at his teaching, for he taught them as one having authority, and not as the scribes. Just then there was in their synagogue a man with an unclean spirit, and he cried out, "What have you to do with us, Jesus of Nazareth? Have you come to destroy us? I know who you are, the Holy One of God." But Jesus rebuked him, saying, "Be silent, and come out of him!" And the unclean spirit, convulsing him and crying with a loud voice, came out of him. They were all amazed, and they kept on asking one another, "What is this? A new teaching—with authority! He commands even the unclean spirits, and they obey him."

—MARK 1:21–27

When You're a Caregiver

HAVE YOU EVER TURNED over in bed on a Sunday morning, groggily remembered church, and groaned, "I'm too tired!" *Too tired to pray?* Your conscience answers you with disbelief, urging you to rise and prepare for prayer. Often that's all you'll need in order to overcome your wish for just a little more sleep.

But the time may well come when "too tired to pray" is a sorrowful reality and not just a wish for another hour of sleep. Most of us have known or will know the dragging weariness of caregiving, helping an ill or disabled parent, spouse, child or friend. Caregiving requires compassion, faith and energy, and sometimes our energy can simply fail us, allowing exhaustion and hopelessness to rear their ugly heads.

What happens when our burdens eat away at prayer? What happens when private time—even privacy itself—becomes only a distant memory? How will it feel when the face we most loved becomes the face we most resent? How will we feel when weariness makes it seem impossible to concentrate on even the basics of life, much less the complex majesty of God?

Some people seem to think that these things don't

happen to believers. Surely our faith will keep us cheerful as we help our loved one. But the rigors of caretaking are as grueling for the devout as they are for everyone else. All caregivers sometimes feel bone-tired trying to anticipate the needs of the person they're caring for. They can experience the wrenching conflict between guilt-ridden love and consuming resentment. Every caregiver knows just how difficult it can be to take care of someone, particularly when the thing we want the most is for someone—anyone—to take care of us. And when the person we're caring for is a friend or relative—perhaps even the parent or spouse who has taken care of us in the past—the sorrow and confusion is sharpened. After all, few families are without conflicts or problems, and the caretaking situation often paints these problems and conflicts in shockingly bold colors.

Even professional caregivers are susceptible to feelings of exhaustion, despair and hopelessness. When I visit my friend Maryann at her nursing home on a weekend, I'm astonished to discover how many of the nurses and aides work double shifts—sixteen hours of feeding, diapering, medicating, washing, exercising, talking to, cajoling and cleaning up after an entire floor of aged or convalescing people. What surprises me more than the rare demonstration of frustration or tired sadness among the staff is the stoic cheer they demonstrate every day and night. Even when their patients dump food trays on the floor or refuse to take medicine, they soldier on bravely.

Those in the caring professions certainly should not be forgotten in any discussion of prayer. Not only do they need and deserve our constant prayers and gratitude, but they also can find themselves too weary and discouraged for their own prayer. When they leave their jobs, they are husbands, wives, parents, children, friends. They also may face the double strain of professional and personal caregiving. It can be easy to abandon any prayer routine in the face of such demands.

In his book *Grace for the Moment*, Max Lucado reminds us that "the greater your cares, the more genuine your prayers. The darker the room, the greater the need for light. God's help is near and always available, but it is only given to those who seek it." And, of course, we all *want* to seek it. However, sometimes we may lack the energy to even know where to start. Whether caregiving is a career or a family obligation, the issues of weariness, emotional fatigue and mental depletion are the same.

The needs and burdens of caregivers are easily overlooked. Even the Bible's most famous caretaker, the Good Samaritan, is only afforded a few lines (Luke 10:30–35). An utter stranger, he risks his own life and spends his own money to rescue, doctor and house a crime victim. That's it: a simple story of a man who never asks for or receives a bit of gratitude—a foreigner without even a name.

But Jesus, recognizing the courage and commitment inherent in caregiving, raised this nameless stranger, a

Samaritan who would be detested by most Jews for his very nation of birth and race, above both a priest and a Levite, revered religious dignitaries. In this way He made it clear that the selfless caregiver was the embodiment of what it meant to follow Him. And in making His caregiver a Samaritan, Jesus suggests that those who may seem to have nothing to offer are capable of giving more than most of us would imagine. They are beloved of the Father and Son because they are doing Their work.

This is the key to the dilemma of prayer for the caregiver: God loves those who care for others. He loves those who offer their minds and backs and muscles and will to people in need, and He understands the magnitude of the task they undertake. He understands the massive burden of caregiving on our frail human nature. So when words fail, when weariness seeps into the brain and drowns the spark of prayer, when the spirit falls flat instead of soaring, the Father understands. So if you are a caregiver, you share in an intimacy with God that can transform the nature of your prayer, if only you perceive it.

To put it simply, as a caregiver, you pray through the act of giving care. Which words express love better than washing the soiled sheets of an invalid? What written prayer is more eloquent than carrying on a seemingly nonsensical conversation with an Alzheimer's victim? What hymn is lovelier than humming softly to try to calm a restless patient? What testimony before an attentive congregation is more pleasing to the ears of God than the patient silence of gently feeding someone who can no longer feed him- or herself?

What transforms your actions as a caregiver into prayer is a simple act of awareness. If you are unable to pray in a traditional manner or attend church, then welcome God into your work and your workplace. Go about your tasks with an awareness of God's presence in and around you. As a caregiver, you are praying in and through your every action. Your work is sacred.

For confirmation of this sanctity of action-as-worship, we need only to turn to that wonderfully pragmatic and tac-iturn disciple, James. The Letter of James, perhaps in part a response to the apostle Paul's more intellectual reliance on faith, emphasizes the need for faith to be expressed in action. James might have been directly addressing caregivers when he writes:

> *My brothers and sisters, whenever you face trials of any kind, consider it nothing but joy, because you know that the testing of your faith produces endurance.*
>
> —JAMES 1:2–3

and:

> *Every generous act of giving, with every perfect gift, is from above, coming down from the Father of lights, with whom there is no variation of shadow due to change.*   —JAMES 1:17

If you think that providing care with a consciousness of God can't be considered prayer, consider these observations of James:

> *If any think they are religious, and do not bridle their tongues but deceive their hearts, their religion is worthless. Religion that is pure and undefiled before God, the Father, is this: to care for orphans and widows in their distress. . . .*   —JAMES 1:26–27

> *What good is it, my brothers and sisters, if you say you have faith but do not have works? Can faith save you? If a brother or sister is naked and lacks daily food, and one of you says to them, "Go in peace; keep warm and eat your fill," and yet you do not supply their bodily needs, what is the good of that? So faith by itself, if it has no works, is dead. . . . Show me your faith without works, and I by my works will show you my faith.*   —JAMES 2:14–18

THE WOUNDED SERVANT

Even the most efficient and kindhearted caregiver is in some way a wounded servant: We are all vulnerable to exhaustion, irritation, sorrow, weakness. We are all human, so we are all wounded by our own nature and by our environment. As a caregiver, a servant—and sometimes a wounded servant—of

God, you should always pray for help in your work, in your humanity, in your woundedness. As you go about your work in silence, these petitions are always before the Lord, yet uttering the words can be a soothing and valuable practice. Upon waking, offer a prayer for help like the following, mentioning the specific needs of the day.

Lord, help me to remember this day that I am doing
Your work.
Give me the patience to do it well;
Give me the grace to be kind;
Give me the energy to continue;
Give my hands the power to lift and work,
the gentleness to comfort and caress,
the flexibility to bring a spoonful of food to trembling lips;
Give my feet the sturdiness to carry me where I must go;
Give my muscles the strength to strip a bed,
turn a patient,
hold a heart;
Give my eyes the clarity to see what is needed
and the tears to show my compassion;
Give my ears the sharpness to hear a soft cry,
a quiet moan,
a whispering breath;
Give my tongue the sweetness to hum, sing,
share a prayer,
speak words of encouragement;

Give my mind peace and calm
and permission to ask for help when I need it;
Give my heart the love to persevere in Your work.

If you're struggling with the burden of caregiving, pray for a change of heart. It's especially hard to care for a family member with whom you've had a difficult history or about whom you have unresolved feelings. When that happens, it's best to admit your weakness and ask for God's help. Again, this petition should be adapted to your personal needs as a caregiver.

Lord, You alone know the extent of my pain,
my exhaustion, my anger.
You know that I sometimes feel I can't go on
carrying this load.
You know that I'm torn between feeling ashamed of myself
and yearning to escape.
Help me, Lord!
Have mercy on me and forgive me.
Teach me what I should do, how I should go on.
When a harsh word comes to my mouth, turn it into a prayer.
When I want to groan or scream, let me sing or hum.
When I see something that looks impossible,
show me how to do it.
When I shrink from a task, fill me with Your spirit
and strength so that I can embrace it.

When I yearn for rest and escape, give my spirit respite and
my body strength.
When my love grows cold, give me Your unconditional
love of others.

We've already discussed the value of repetition in prayer, especially when prayer is difficult. If you're a caregiver, lengthy prayers may seem impossible, particularly during a busy day of work. It may be useful for you to simply repeat a portion or line of a prayer that particularly expresses your feelings and your own situation. You can use a portion of the prayers above or develop your own personal prayer statements. You may find it helpful to repeat some simple prayer-declarations and prayer-supplications throughout the day, like these:

Lord, let me remember that I am doing Your work.

Lord, help me!

Lord, give me Your love!

Lord, show me what I should do.

THE HURTING HEALER

Jesus has been referred to as the Hurting Healer because, although He cured all who came to Him and ultimately healed the whole world, He did so at great cost. He suffered brutally, endlessly and not only during the violent hours of

His trial, beatings and execution. Always "on call," Jesus showed very human signs of exhaustion, of needing to recover, after He'd given too much of Himself. Witness how often He instructed those He'd healed to tell no one.

> *Once . . . there was a man covered with leprosy. When he saw Jesus, he bowed with his face to the ground and begged him, "Lord, if you choose, you can make me clean." Then Jesus stretched out his hand, touched him, and said, "I do choose. Be made clean." Immediately the leprosy left him. And he ordered him to tell no one. . . . But now more than ever the word about Jesus spread abroad; many crowds would gather to hear him and to be cured of their diseases. But he would withdraw to deserted places and pray.*
>
> —LUKE 5:12–16

It's almost as if He couldn't take one more demand, one more tiring encounter. Indeed, Jesus knew what was coming and must have at times felt reluctant to even begin the work He knew would be frustrating, wearying, painful and ultimately, literally, His death.

Jesus hurt in His heart as well as in His body. He grieved for those He'd come to save, for the entire nation, for those He would ultimately lose because they would not hear or believe in Him. We hear Him speak of Jerusalem and its people as if describing a sick patient whom He yearns to heal no matter the cost to Himself:

"Jerusalem, Jerusalem ...! How often have I desired to gather your children together as a hen gathers her brood under her wings, and you were not willing!"

—MATTHEW 23:37

Jesus suffered personally as well for His ministry. We can only imagine His pain when he was told about the murder of His cousin John the Baptist.

Now when Jesus heard this, he withdrew from there in a boat to a deserted place by himself. But when the crowds heard it, they followed him on foot from the towns. When he went ashore, he saw a great crowd; and he had compassion for them and cured their sick.

—MATTHEW 14:13–14

How deeply did Jesus desire to take the time to mourn for John, to nurse His own sorrow and loss? Yet He girded Himself again and went out to meet the needs of those who sought Him.

And all this is to say nothing of Jesus' emotional, physical and spiritual suffering during the twenty-four hours before His death. He faced the grief of parting from His beloved disciples, the humiliation of being mocked and scorned by His own people, the searing pain of the whip on His back, the piercing of the thorns and nails, the agony of hanging for hours on a cross as He slowly suffocated.

Jesus certainly deserves to be honored as our Hurting Healer, both in the manner of His life and His death. Most of us will never comprehend the magnitude of His anguish, but perhaps in your suffering as caregivers, you can find a way to identify—and through your actions, pray—with Jesus. When you wash a bedridden person, see Jesus' torn and filthy body and move the warm cloth gently. When you comb his or her hair, picture Jesus' tangled curls clotted with blood and dirt. When you try to coax a few drops of soup through the cracked and dry lips of a sick person, think about Jesus taking liquid from the sponge soaked with wine. When you're feeding a hungry patient a morsel of food, recall how Jesus fed His disciples with His body and blood just hours before He gave Himself up to be abused and crucified. When you exercise atrophied arms and legs, remember how Jesus' limbs were respectfully arranged by weeping attendants in the repose of death. When you're changing bedclothes, envision the clean cloths that were carefully wrapped around Jesus' body.

When you hear a groan, remember that "Jesus cried with a loud voice, 'My God, my God, why have you forsaken me?'" (Matthew 27:46), and rush to soothe your patient. When you hear labored breathing, think about how those gathered around Jesus listened to Him gasping for breath as His chest and lungs collapsed on the cross. When you change a bandage, picture the women at the tomb anointing and binding Jesus' many wounds. When you help prepare someone for death, you join the women and men who waited faithfully at the foot of the cross, never letting Jesus feel alone.

Respite

Jesus both offered and took respite. We all know the Scriptures in which He urges us to come to Him and rest, and we must heed that call. But we read in the Gospels that when healing power had gone out of Him, the Lord Himself needed respite, to withdraw from the crowds and turn inward, to His Father. Perhaps He sometimes surprised or even dismayed the followers who felt He should be constantly accessible to them. In the same way, you may surprise and disappoint those who rely on you to be always "on call" as a caregiver. During these times, you can take strength and consolation from Jesus' example.

Jesus' need for respite is evident throughout Scripture. On one occasion He dismisses a crowd and sends His disciples away across the lake in a boat.

> *After saying farewell to them, he went up on the mountain to pray. When evening came, the boat was out on the lake, and he was alone on the land. When he saw that they were straining at the oars against an adverse wind, he came towards them early in the morning, walking on the lake. He intended to pass them by.*
>
> —MARK 6:46–48

Even then, as they struggled in the storm on the lake, He wanted to pass them by so He could remain alone. But He didn't, because He knew they were suffering and might perish without His help.

Jesus' wish for respite was loud and clear during one healing:

> *When they came to the crowd, a man came to him, knelt before him, and said, "Lord, have mercy on my son, for he . . . suffers terribly; he often falls into the fire and often into the water. And I brought him to your disciples, but they could not cure him." Jesus answered, "You faithless and perverse generation, how much longer must I be with you? How much longer must I put up with you? Bring him here to me." And . . . the boy was cured instantly.*   —MATTHEW 17:14–18

Jesus does not hesitate to express His irritation, and yet He does not punish the child for the failings of faith in the adults.

This pattern appears over and over again. While on His way to one healing, He is accosted by a crowd, and as He struggles to pass through them so that He can reach the house where a dying child waits, a desperate woman reaches out and touches His cloak in order to be healed.

> *Immediately aware that power had gone forth from him, Jesus turned about in the crowd and said, "Who touched my clothes?" . . . He looked all round to see who had done it. But the woman, knowing what had happened to her, came in fear and trembling, fell down before him, and told him the whole truth. He said to her, "Daughter, your faith has made you well; go in peace, and be healed. . . ."*   —MARK 5:29–30, 32–34

In both of these cases, we can see a moment where Jesus has just about had it with all the demands placed on Him. In the latter case, He seems surprised that someone has dared to steal a cure from Him without the courtesy of even asking! But when He sees the woman, His weariness evaporates, and He commends her faith and declares her healed.

What are we to make of these demonstrations of Jesus' weariness and need for rest? Only that He too, as we often forget, was human! As a man, He needed rest from the enormous burdens He bore. And He didn't feel ashamed of His need for respite—He expressed those feelings and desires quite clearly. Nor did He feel guilty when He took time away. Though our burdens are much smaller, we are even more susceptible to exhaustion, vexation and sorrow. Still, we can use our times of respite, as Jesus did, to seek a stronger bond with the Father.

Before you lie down to rest, thank the Father for this time of sleep. Ask Him to bless your sleep and your dreams and to let you wake refreshed to resume your work. Use your respite period to pray silently through imaging and meditation. As Jesus did, go to a quiet place to commune with the Father. Jesus often went to secluded places—mountains, seashores, gardens—to spend time with the Father. You too can find suitable places that are conducive to peace, rest and prayer. Once there and once relaxed as much as possible, you can pray in any number of ways. Simply "being" with the Father seemed to work well for Jesus, and we would do well to follow that model.

While resting in the Father's presence, you might focus on images of your own body and spirit being healed by the Father and the Son and the Holy Spirit. Imagine cleansing water being poured over you, washing away the anxiety and exhaustion and even cynicism that weigh you down. Envision the light of the Lord shining on you and feel it warming your weary body. Breathe the air and know that it is yours, the space you are in is yours, and you are alone with God. No one can make a demand upon you in these moments. Picture your heart being mended, your brain renewed, your muscles strengthened. Sleep!

Jesus also took respite with others, and no caregiver should pass up an opportunity to enjoy life. Indeed, for the caregiver, these opportunities are all too rare and should be embraced whenever possible. Accept an invitation to a meal, lavish or simple; share a cup of coffee with a friend; read; attend a church festival; join a book group; participate in a Bible study; eat fruit from the tree or the vine; take a long walk through a park or some farmland; go to a wedding; tell your friends that you love them. Respite does not have to be a Caribbean vacation. (Though that's not a bad idea, if possible!) It can be as short as an hour, or as long as it takes. All of these, any of these, are respite.

THANKSGIVING

These prayers of thanksgiving are designed to help caregivers and those who are exhausted from their burdens. They are suggestions; feel free to alter them according to your need, and remember that you don't have to limit yourself to these few words.

Creator of all, thank You for giving us the Sabbath as a reminder that even You took a day of rest from all Your labor.

All-knowing Jesus, thank You for instructing me to take my rest in You and for welcoming me when I feel weary.

Understanding Lord, thank You for those in my life and community who recognize my burdens and communicate their empathy to me.

Dear God, thank You for giving me compassion, patience and strength even when I feel tired and fragile.

Loving Father, thank You for the rest I am able to take and for those who provide me with hope and respite.

Jesus, thank You for showing me that it is okay to take time apart to rest and be with You.

Lord, let me rise from rest ready to do Your work.

Psalm-as-Prayer

As a caregiver, you need nothing as much as hope—and rest. This psalm recognizes what you are up against—the constant demands of others—and encourages you to be patient and take your rest in the Lord. It assures you that God, Who sees and recompenses all, is always close by. It promises comfort and divine recognition for your pains.

PSALM 37:1–9
EXHORTATION TO PATIENCE AND TRUST

Do not fret because of the wicked;
do not be envious of wrongdoers,
for they will soon fade like the grass,
and wither like the green herb.
Trust in the Lord, and do good;
so you will live in the land, and enjoy security.
Take delight in the Lord,
and he will give you the desires of your heart.
Commit your way to the Lord;
trust in him, and he will act.
He will make your vindication shine like the light,
and the justice of your cause like the noonday.
Be still before the Lord, and wait patiently for him;
do not fret over those who prosper in their way,
over those who carry out evil devices.
Refrain from anger, and forsake wrath.
Do not fret—it leads only to evil.
For the wicked shall be cut off,
but those who wait for the Lord shall inherit the land.

Suggested Closing Prayer

Jesus, my brother, I believe You understand my exhaustion, even my frustration and resentment. Though the Son of God, You made Yourself human; and so You must have felt the same human emotions I sometimes feel. Please forgive me, Lord, and help me to feel that forgiveness. Help me to forgive myself. Stay close to me in my daily work, and teach me to recognize You in those I seek to help. Give me energy when I am weary, and let me sleep easily when I rest. Oh, Lord, lend me Your patience, Your strength, Your presence!

Bible Reference

All spoke well of him and were amazed at the gracious words that came from his mouth. They said, "Is not this Joseph's son?" He said to them, "Doubtless you will quote to me this proverb, 'Doctor, cure yourself!' And you will say, 'Do here also in your home town the things that we have heard you did at Capernaum.'" And he said, "Truly I tell you, no prophet is accepted in the prophet's hometown." —LUKE 4:22–24

When You're Mourning

PEOPLE IN DEEP MOURNING are among those most likely to give up on prayer. When you mourn, you may feel as though you've lost everything. You may think that your prayers for the well-being and healing of the one you've lost were not answered. The comfort you may take from knowing that your loved one has gone to God can easily be overshadowed by the pain you're feeling for your loss here and now. When you experience this kind of rending grief, how do you stay close to God? How can you find the voice to call His name?

Sometimes we grieve profoundly for the loss of someone who is still living. Ask any parent mourning for a child who has become a stranger because he or she is addicted to drugs or is in a destructive relationship. Ask a child whose parent has abandoned the family. Ask a spouse who is grieving for the end of a marriage. A woman in my church who recently went through a divorce told me, "I've lost my husband, and I've lost my marriage. This is a deeper sorrow than what I might have experienced if death had ended a long, happy marriage."

Even more difficult is the grief that comes when a loved one has been taken from us suddenly by an accident or an act of violence. It can take even longer for grief to give way to peace and recovery than in the case of natural death. In these trying situations, uttering words of prayer may not be as important as seeking to stay close to God, to simply put ourselves in a place where God's silent presence can be our prayer.

Our mourning is not really for the dead; it is for us, the living, and the pain we experience at the death or the loss of a loved one. Jesus knew this. When He heard that His friend Lazarus was dying, Jesus delayed going to Lazarus and his sisters Martha and Mary. He knew that He had to let Lazarus die so that He could then raise him up. Yet when Jesus meets Martha and Mary, observing firsthand their grief and that of all the friends who had gathered to grieve with them, He finds their sorrow almost unbearable.

> [Martha] went back and called her sister Mary, and told her privately, "The Teacher is here and is calling for you." And when she heard it she got up quickly and went to him. . . . When Mary came where Jesus was and saw him, she knelt at his feet and said to him, "Lord, if you had been here, my brother would not have died." When Jesus saw her weeping, and the Jews who came with her also weeping, he was greatly disturbed in spirit and deeply moved. . . . Jesus began to weep. So the Jews said, "See how he loved him!" But some of them said, "Could not he who opened the eyes of the blind man have kept this man from dying?"
>
> —JOHN 11:28–37

They didn't understand. Jesus wasn't weeping because He missed Lazarus; after all, He knew He was about to raise him from death. And Jesus wasn't weeping because He had healed others and not His own friend—after all, He was about to turn all this sorrow to joy. So why did Jesus weep? Because He understood and felt the magnitude of the grief experienced by Martha and Mary and Lazarus' friends. Jesus fully comprehends our agony at the death of a loved one. He grieves with us.

There were other occasions in which Jesus raised the dead, apparently because He was so moved by the grief and faith of those who loved them. In Mark 5:35–43, we witness Jesus enduring ridicule and attracting the attention of the religious hierarchy by raising the daughter of Jairus, a leader of the local synagogue. He ignores the would-be mourners who laugh at Him when He says that the girl is not dead, and then raises the child with just a few words. It is almost as if He cannot ignore the sorrow of her parents and must do what is in His power to eradicate it, despite the scorn of others and the risk to Himself.

In Luke's Gospel, Jesus seems to have no reason to raise the only son of a widow besides sheer compassion for the heartbroken woman. He does not even ask for a show of her faith as He did with Jairus and Martha and Mary; and the widow herself seems to have no idea who He is.

As he approached the gate of the town, a man who had died was being carried out. He was his mother's only son, and she was a widow; and with her was a large crowd from the town. When the Lord saw her, he had compassion for her and said to her, "Do not weep." Then he came forward and touched the bier, and the bearers stood still. And he said, "Young man, I say to you, rise!" The dead man sat up and began to speak, and Jesus gave him to his mother.   —LUKE 7:12–15

Time and again, Scripture shows us that the Lord comprehends the abyss of human grief, and yet in our own grief, we often forget how deeply God commiserates with us. In this we are very much like Jesus' own followers: We lose sight of both God's power *and* what it means to die and go to the Lord. When the disciples thought Jesus had died forever on the cross, they were paralyzed, speechless with sorrow and fear at being left alone, separate from the One on whom their lives depended. They were petrified and despairing, as if they had forgotten everything He'd done, everything He was capable of, and everything He'd told them about the kingdom of Heaven and the Holy Spirit Who would come to them.

And after Jesus' ascension, even though the disciples had seen and talked and touched and eaten with their resurrected Lord, they fell again into fear and paralysis. One Pentecost, my pastor addressed the grief of the disciples. He noted that even after all they had seen, all they had experienced, all they had come to believe about Jesus, they were still bereft and

afraid after He left them. Not long after the agony they felt at
the crucifixion and the joy they felt at the Resurrection, they
still slipped back into mourning His absence. "They were
paralyzed and afraid," he said, "hiding still from the Jews. And
then there were tongues of fire and a rushing wind, and the
Spirit of the Lord came upon them. And they were speaking
in tongues and different languages, so that everyone present
from other regions and countries could understand them in
his or her own language. They were filled with the Holy
Spirit, and they were no longer afraid because they now had
a constant reminder that Jesus was with them always, and
that they would be going to join Him eventually. They went
from feeling paralyzed to feeling alive with the energy to
organize and build the church."

If you've mourned the death of a loved one, you're familiar with this sense of paralysis. But are you also familiar with
the indwelling of the Spirit, the infusion of energy and life
and hope that is Christ's presence and Christ's reassurance?
Jesus sent the Spirit to the disciples on Pentecost to wipe
away their grief and paralysis, to comfort them with the
reminder that He was with them no matter what happened.
That same Spirit is accessible to you too as you mourn. He is
present with you, the living proof that death is but a temporary separation. Though you may not be ready to pray,
though you may not immediately feel the consolation in
this, it is true consolation.

And this consolation can become prayer for those who

mourn. When praying with words does not seem possible, you can meditate on the gift of the Spirit, perhaps reading appropriate Scriptures as encouragement. You needn't worry if your meditations don't immediately blossom into prayer; you can simply allow these thoughts into your mind and let them rest there as long as possible. For those who mourn, these meditations are a valid form of prayer and the beginning of a journey from paralysis to comprehension to life. Think of Jesus' compassion and His power over death:

- Jesus wept at Lazarus' grave because He saw and felt the impact of grief on Martha and Mary and their friends.

- Though the religious leaders who were Jesus' enemies would surely learn of it, and though bystanders mocked Him, Jesus was so understanding of grieving parents that He raised the small daughter of Jairus, a synagogue leader, from the dead.

- Jesus had so much compassion for the widow of Nain that He raised her only son from the dead even though no one had even appealed to Him for help.

- Jesus understands grief. He knew how desperately His own followers would grieve for Him and sent them the Holy Spirit to comfort and encourage them.

Meditations like these are prayers in and of themselves and they may also lead you to pray with words. The following simple prayers can be helpful when you feel so moved.

Lord, I know that You comprehend the depth of my grief. Please, Lord, take some of this pain from me, for I cannot bear it all alone. Please give me the grace to relinquish my sorrow to You, bit by bit, as I am ready. And then, Lord, fill my empty spaces in whatever ways are best for me.

Father, You allowed Your own Son to be given up to death. As I grieve, I take comfort in knowing that You have grieved long before I have. This pain is something we share. Take me in Your arms, Lord, and help me turn from this grief to life.

Lord, You comforted Your followers and established the church by sending Your Spirit to those who mourned Your loss. I beg You, Lord, send me Your Spirit now! Comfort me with Your presence, for in Your presence I know I will feel the love You have for my lost loved one. In You, all who love You will be reunited. Let me be filled with Your Spirit now so that I am no longer an empty vessel, but one that holds hope and grace.

Many Paths

A friend who went through the horrifying experience of losing his young son in an accident had a request for me. It was shortly after the public mourning period, the first few weeks of visits and calling hours and services. There were fewer people around him then, fewer diversions from the reality of life without his boy. Our friend had pretty much had it with ill-expressed good intentions and just plain curiosity, and he and his family were just then awakening to a deeper grief.

"The next time you write a book about faith," he asked, "make sure you tell people never, *never*, to tell a parent that the child they just lost is 'better off where he is now.' Tell people never to say that! They don't know what they're talking about. They don't know how that feels!"

He's right. Though we mean well when we say such things, most of us simply can't know how it feels to hear such a statement. How does it sound to a parent who can't begin to imagine that a beloved child could be better off anywhere but with his parents and the rest of his family? At such a time in the journey of grief, it is hard for parents to feel that their child is better off even with God.

Several years ago a television movie was made about the life of Christ, the first third focusing on His birth and childhood with Mary and Joseph. It went into great depth depicting the likely relationship between these extraordinary parents and their even more extraordinary Son, recreating the Nativity, the flight into Egypt, and the presentation of the baby Jesus at the temple, when both the prophetess Anna and the holy man Simeon proclaimed with much praise that the Infant was the Messiah.

During all these scenes, mostly taken from the Gospel of

Luke, Joseph and Mary are depicted as deeply loving parents who are not a little troubled and burdened by what they come to know about their child. You can almost see them flinch when Simeon, after taking the Infant in his arms, proclaims, "This child is destined for the falling and the rising of many in Israel, and to be the sign that will be opposed so that the inner thoughts of many will be revealed—and a sword will pierce your own soul too" (Luke 2:34–35).

Joseph in particular seems to gird himself to be a real father to this boy, regardless of the cost to himself. Joseph teaches Jesus carpentry, he oversees His education, he brings Him to the synagogue, all as any loving Jewish father would have done. Both Joseph and Mary are shown as frantic when the twelve-year-old Jesus is thought to be lost at the temple in Jerusalem after the Passover festival. In the scene where Joseph's death is imagined on film, we see both Jesus and Mary grieving deeply with the actress portraying Mary, the much younger wife of a man who has protected and cared for her since her own childhood, appearing to be lost in sorrow for the man who was father, husband, brother and friend to her.

Later when we see an only slightly older Mary at the foot of the cross, the movie takes a turn I'd never seen before. This Mary seems to feel every pain, every humiliation, every agony with her Son on the cross. She is far from the calm, quietly suffering mother we've come to know from Hollywood films. When He struggles for breath, she seems to be suffocating. When He tries to shift His broken body to ease the pain, she wraps her arms around herself as if to squeeze away her own pain. She cannot take her eyes off of Him, and when He dies and is laid in her arms, she clutches His ruined body to hers, falling to the muddy ground, and then she opens her mouth wide and simply wails. She lifts her face to the dark storm that is now thundering all around them, and she shrieks out her grief. Even this mother, this mother who knows more than any of us, this mother who was chosen by the Father to carry His Son, this mother with all her wisdom and experience, cannot at first seem to believe that her Son is in "a better place." All she knows at that moment is that He is gone from her.

The movie was shown over several evenings. The day after it ended, I called my grandmother, then in her early nineties. I knew she'd been watching; she was attracted to all things religious, and this movie would not have escaped her attention. After we talked about the movie for a bit, I said, "Mary at the Cross really surprised me. I'd never seen anything like that in a movie about Jesus. Even though I don't have any kids, I really understood what she was feeling. No one has ever shown her shrieking in anguish like that, but you know, I got to thinking that she probably *did* feel just that devastated."

My grandmother was indignant at my surprise. "Of course she felt that way!" she said impatiently. "What else would she have felt?" I guess Hollywood had finally understood what every parent knows.

If Mary did indeed mourn her Son with cries and anguish, as most parents would, are we to believe that God was disappointed at her reaction? Is God distressed with us when we mourn? Does He see our paralyzing grief as a lack of faith? Perhaps the best answer I've heard to this question also came from television in the form and voice of a preacher on what in my region is called the Worship Channel, a cable television channel that offers prayers, music and short talks by various ministers and preachers.

In this particular segment the young preacher was speaking about grief. He told the story of a friend who'd lost a child to disease. The friend at first was frozen with sorrow, but when the ice melted, the first thing he felt was anger toward God. He was furious that God, Whom he trusted and loved, had taken his child. I suspect that many who grieve feel this way; in fact, anger is an identified stage in the grieving process. Still, most of us might not easily admit that we are angry with God. This father apparently had no qualms in not only admitting it, but expressing it. He was, it seems, no Abraham willing to sacrifice his son for his faith.

Yet as the preacher pointed out, the father was expressing profound faith every time he expressed his anger and sorrow to God. The father kept talking to *his* Father *in spite of* his sorrow, anger, frustration. Could there be a greater sign of faith than to maintain a conversation with God after such a loss? Just by the act of expressing himself to God, that parent was saying, "Even as I grieve and feel angry, I know You're there. I know You hear me. I trust You to understand what I feel. I trust You to understand my anger and grief."

From those statements—which are surely prayers—it's not such a long way toward acknowledging that the child who had gone to such an omniscient, forgiving and loving God is indeed in a wonderful place.

Can bringing your anger, sorrow, paralysis and sense of abandonment to God truly be a form of prayer? Of course. Prayer is a conversation with God, and it assumes that God hears us even when we may not be ready to admit it. Or as the preacher concluded, "It's okay to be upset with God. He can take it. And that's the important thing to know: that God is big enough to take our anger." And together with God, in talking to God, you will transform that anger and sorrow into prayer.

On what initially seems to be the opposite end of the grief spectrum is my friend Ruby. Ruby, who says she is twenty-one because she was born on February 29 of a long-ago leap year, had Quaker grandparents and is herself a member of a mission church. She has a deep and profoundly simple faith. She professes to be perplexed by all the anguish that surrounds death. "If we are truly Christians, why do we mourn so bitterly for our loved ones?" she asks. "If we are believers, we know that they are safe with God and no longer suffering. Why don't we rejoice?"

Ruby has nursed and buried her mother, her father, her brother (who was blind) and her best friend, whom she took in when the woman became ill with cancer. She is well-acquainted with death and the period of loss that follows the death of a loved one. She has carefully planned her own funeral since she has a dread of what she considers excessive and maudlin rituals. "I'm relieved to have all that done," she assures me, letting me know that she doesn't wish me or anyone to grieve terribly for her. Then she adds with a mischievous half smile, "I'm ready. I'm just not in a big hurry."

WAITING

None of us are in a big hurry to face death—not our own, and certainly not the death of a loved one. But although death doesn't wait for the time we choose, we must wait out our grief. Grief, like death, takes its own time, and it is during this time of waiting that prayer can be both a way of continuing to communicate with God and a tool for healing. Much has been made of identifying the stages of grief, and while people may disagree about whether everyone goes through every stage, it's fair to say that everyone who grieves experiences some of the same emotions.

Grief is a waiting period, the time it takes for us to fully experience our loss and begin to heal, and the time needed and the degree to which each or any of these feelings manifest themselves will be different for everyone. Some of us may take a longer time than others to pass through the stages of bereavement. Some of us may be more emotional, showing our feelings more than others. Some of us may stay in, secluding ourselves, while others prefer to be out, working and maintaining our routine. Respect the process, both in yourself and in others. Avoiding judgmental thinking and comparisons about how you or someone else experiences grief is an important step toward healing. After a significant loss, feelings of disbelief or numbness, anger (both at God and at everything associated with the loss—including the loved one), abandonment, loneliness and confusion are all common.

Though it may seem difficult, it is possible to pray through each of these emotions. Even if you can't manage conventional prayer, there are ways to stay in touch with God as you pass through your personal period of mourning. First it is important to explore which of your feelings are strongest at any given time. You may be experiencing more than one of the grief emotions at the same time. This is typical, and often adds to the sense of desolation and confusion in the wake of losing a loved one.

As you prepare to pray, try to identify the feeling that is having the greatest impact on you. If your predominant emotion is disbelief or numbness, you can try praying like this:

Lord, I cannot take in what has happened.
I feel paralyzed, unable to accept this devastating blow.
At times I can't even believe that my beloved is lost to me.
Lord, waken me out of this cold paralysis.
Though I realize that awareness will bring pain,
let me fully understand the reality of my loss.
Replace my coldness first with comprehension and then
with the warmth of Your comfort. Keep me close to You, Lord,
as I confront this sorrow, my sorrow.

I have already talked about feeling angry with God after a loss, but you may be feeling other types of anger. The targets may include doctors or other health-care workers, relatives and friends, work colleagues, neighbors, and, as I noted above, even the person who has been lost. Though such anger may be very real and very disturbing, it is not always appropriate. For example, rage at a doctor who has done all she could, anger at an associate who seems to be intrusive but is only concerned, fury at a relative who does not seem to show grief but is privately devastated, resentment at the person who is gone simply because you feel he or she has left you behind—all of these may be deeply and honestly felt without necessarily being fair or even right. But at this stage, fairness is not really the point. Experiencing and understanding the anger is the point.

Part of getting over that anger is expressing it to God.

A trusting conversation with God about such feelings can be a cleansing prayer. For example:

Father, my anger is overwhelming.
It seems to be as strong as my sadness.
I feel that it is consuming me, keeping me from You
and from healing.
Cleanse me, Father, from my anger.
Let me feel the sorrow that I know is deep within me
without the heat of rage.
Show me how to work through my anger,
so that I can be calm enough to recognize what I truly feel.
Help me to forgive those with whom I am angry.
Help them to forgive me.
And Lord, forgive me as well.
Help me to be patient with myself,
trusting in Your grace to cleanse me.

Many people feel abandoned as part of their sorrow. Such a feeling may be connected to the nature of their relationship with the person who is gone, or it may simply be a natural part of the grieving process. If you were dependent on the one you've lost, or felt abandoned early in life by a parent, sibling or other key figure, you may suddenly experience such feelings all over again. In some cases you may feel that the people in your life who knew your loved one have abandoned you too. This may be your imagination, or it may be painfully true that the people who have cared about you in the past simply feel uncomfortable with you now. Naturally this leaves you feeling betrayed and lonely. You may even feel abandoned by God. And sometimes just the fear of abandonment can be paralyzing, making prayer difficult.

If you can't find your own words to express these feelings to God, you can try praying:

> *Always-present Lord, I feel that I've been abandoned.*
> *I have had this sense before in my life, but this time*
> *it feels overwhelming.*
> *I feel that the loved one I've lost has abandoned me,*
> *and I worry that others in my life will abandon me.*
> *I even wonder if You have abandoned me.*
> *Comfort me,*
> *Remind me that You never abandon those who love You*
> *and turn to You as I am doing.*
> *From Job, to Naomi,*
> *from the Canaanite woman who begged for her daughter*
> *to be healed only to receive*
> *Jesus' initial rebuff,*
> *to Peter, who must have felt abandoned*
> *when he denied his Lord,*
> *so many of Your faithful followers have felt abandoned*
> *at one time or another.*
> *Yet You have always proved true, Lord.*

Reveal Your presence to me now and take away
my feelings of abandonment.

With bereavement comes loneliness. No matter how many— or few—friends and relatives are available, you feel alone, without the one you've come to love and need. There is an acute sense of what has been lost, and this is often accompanied by a belief that it cannot be replaced. These feelings are perfectly valid and realistic. Something vital *has* been lost, and it cannot be replaced, at least not in the form it took. There will not be another person precisely like the one you've lost. There will not be another presence in your life precisely like that presence.

None of this means that God wants you to give in to the despair of loneliness. Our God is a God of hope. There are other people in your life and other people who will come into your life if and when you are ready to welcome them. Most important, God is with you, even in those most poignant times of loneliness. To recognize the Presence from Whom all good things come, you might pray:

Lord, I have been taught that You are Father, Brother,
Best Friend.
Let me feel Your presence in all these ways, because, Lord,
I feel so alone now.
I miss my lost one so deeply that it is physical agony!
I yearn for the sound of that familiar voice, the touch
of that gentle hand,

the conversations we enjoyed, the laughter, the tears,
the meals we shared, all of it, Lord!
Help me to understand that I must accept these feelings,
without succumbing to them. Teach me, Lord,
that by turning toward You,
Father, Brother, Best Friend,
I am turning away from my loneliness.
Remind me that You brought my lost one into my life, and
You will bring others—not to take my beloved's place,
but to ease my loneliness and show me the way forward.
Give me the grace to open myself to You and to the people
You bring into my life.
When I'm alone, guide my thoughts
to the happy memories of the times I shared
with my lost loved one.
Remind me that You will bring us together again.

Confusion is likely to plague every stage and phase and feeling associated with bereavement. This is natural, and it has many causes. The exhaustion and anxiety that accompany a loss can easily result in feelings of uncertainty and confusion. It becomes difficult to focus or to understand what is happening. There may even be times when you forget that your loved one is lost to us.

Not long ago, I attended the funeral of my ninety-five-year-old grandmother. My husband Charlie and I had just flown back home to Connecticut from Florida after being away over a month. It was the middle of winter, and we had barely unpacked and accustomed ourselves to the dim light, long nights and cold climate of Connecticut. My family, most of whom I hadn't seen since Christmas, were gathered in the back of the church—parents, sister and brother-in-law, aunt, cousins, close friends, all the people I would have seen around my grandmother at a picnic or a birthday party. Without even thinking, I turned to my sister Lori and asked, "Where's Nana?"

As soon as the words were out, I realized what I'd said. But Lori's eyes grew wide with recognition and before I could say another word, she replied, "I know! I was thinking the same thing."

There are things that may confuse you during the grieving process. If the person you've lost had been in charge of financial matters and the daily paperwork, you may suddenly be faced with a raft of documents and decisions that may need to be dealt with immediately. It's difficult enough to manage these matters when you are familiar with them, never mind in the midst of grief. While a trusted advisor can be invaluable, too much advice during such a time can just add to the uncertainty when it comes to making important decisions.

When you mourn, you can also become confused by the variety of strong emotions you experience, sometimes for the first time. Why do you suddenly feel angry with the one you have lost? How can you feel both resentment and deep yearning at the same time? How can you face the future when you have no idea what it holds? Why has this happened? Why has God let it happen? How can you function without answers, without clarity, without any idea of what will happen in the future?

As time passes, you may also be disturbed when you experience the first emotions not directly associated with your loss. You can feel confused and even guilty the first time you feel hungry for a certain favorite food, laugh heartily at a joke or a movie, awaken and look forward to the day, and especially the first time you feel close to another person.

How should you pray through and about your confusion? As simply and directly as possible. Prayer should help you, not add another confusing burden. You may try praying like this:

Father, I am tired, mixed up, and sad.
I feel dim and sluggish, surrounded by chaos and uncertainty.
My world has been turned inside out, and I just
don't know what to do.
Please help me, Lord!
Surround me with Your love and let the light
of Your Presence pierce the dusk around me.
Let me understand that what I feel is perfectly natural
and that when I am able to handle the future,
You will reveal it to me.

ACTIVE PRAYER

You can meet your grief with active prayer as well as spoken prayer. The actions you take become prayer simply because they are touched by the love of God and your own desire to move through the mourning process. Active prayer through mourning is a way of working with God to bring about the healing. Active prayer then becomes a loving, trusting expression of hope just when you may feel most unhopeful.

Many years ago I became friends with a woman who had recently lived through an extended depression. This was long before many carefully formulated medications were available for those living with depression. In those days, the only drugs available had serious side effects, often making the patient feel exhausted, nauseated and slow-witted.

"I didn't want to turn into a zombie, and that's what I felt like just a week or so into the medication," my friend recalled, "so I decided to try to take action for myself. I just didn't know what else to do. It wasn't easy! Often I didn't want to do anything except stay in bed with the shades drawn. But I forced myself to do certain things every day. First, just get up. Get dressed. Make the bed. Later, I made myself spend at least a few hours working. I would respond with a smile and a few words to at least one person who spoke to me every day. These things sound so small, but they were so difficult for me at the time.

"After a while something surprising happened. I started doing some of these things without thinking about them. They became part of my routine. At the end of one particular day I realized that not only had I responded to more than one person that day, but I'd actually greeted someone first! Without forcing it. That was really a turning point for me. I began to feel that by going through the motions of living, I could actually start living again."

To take such action in the context of faith and in the presence of God is active prayer. Practical action like the program followed by my depressed friend becomes prayer when we invite God to join and guide us, and when we take action in an effort to help return to a state of spiritual health. As you work through your grief, you may want to consider the following prayer-actions:

Write a letter. Writing is a good way to express your feelings, even if—perhaps especially if—no one except for God will ever see the letter. When you feel angry, sad, confused, bereft, abandoned, lonely or any other emotion associated with mourning, you can write a letter to God, detailing your emotion and asking for help.

Before you start writing, ask God to help you write clearly and honestly. Ask Him to be attentive to the letter and the feelings it expresses. Begin the letter, "My dear Father," or "My dear Lord," and end it with "Amen" and your name.

Write as often as you find it helpful—every day, if you feel called to. Read your letter again at the end of the day and then keep it as a future prayer resource.

You may also find it helpful to write a letter to the one you've lost, obviously not so that the person can read it, but to express your many emotions about the loss. This can be an active prayer for healing and resolution, and here again, the letters should be honest in order to better cleanse the heart. Before beginning the letter, ask God for the courage to write what you need to communicate and to let you be conscious of His healing power. While writing, hold the image of your loved one in your heart and mind and just let your words flow. Here too, it may be helpful to write more than one letter and to keep and reread them.

Writing a letter to a living person who is involved in your grieving process can also help move you toward resolution of your grief. You can write to someone who shares your grief, someone with whom you are angry or frustrated, or someone who didn't know your loved one very well in life and would like to know more. Clearly the content of each of these letters will vary: If you write to someone who shares your grief, your letter will cover common ground and even celebrate memories. If you are writing to someone with whom you are upset, your letter might describe the problem and your feelings about it. If you're writing to a person who might want to know more about your loved one, the letter might be a wonderful testament, recounting stories and memories. Regardless of whom you write to, you are affirming your place in the life God gave you and implicitly showing your respect for His plan for you. Before beginning this letter, ask God for the skill to write clearly, the compassion to see the other person's perspective, and the courage to express honest feelings. Ask God to guide the letter so that the recipient may be blessed with understanding. Read the letter after you've written it; if you believe it may have a hurtful impact on the recipient, you can choose not to send it. You can simply keep it as a chronicle of your feelings.

Join a bereavement or grief support group. This positive prayer-action is a particularly good option if the group is run or recommended by those in a faith-based or church community. People who are grieving need to be with those who truly understand, and no one can understand better than those who have experienced the same emotions. If you can't find an appropriate support group, you might consider starting your own, even if it just has one or two other members at first.

If you're technologically proficient, you might want to explore Internet connections with individuals or groups working with the grief process. This involves a certain amount of research and some discernment, but it has proven extremely helpful for groups like the families of soldiers in

Iraq who can connect with people who know exactly how they feel.

In preparing to attend or contact a bereavement group, ask God to be with you, guide your participation, and teach you to listen as well as contribute.

Pray with the words of another. There are many books and essays about grief. You may find it helpful to find that someone else has felt what you are feeling. And while no two people mourn in the same way, you may find comfort in the words of someone who has gone through deep sorrow.

Confess to God. We know that if we confess our sins and failings to God, He will forgive us and give us a new start. People in mourning sometimes forget the important cleansing process of confession. "What do I have to confess?" you may ask. "Am I not the one who's been wronged, alone, bereft? What sin have I committed?"

The answers to these questions—if you are honest—may surprise you. Have you been angry with your loved one or someone else? Have you been angry with God? Have you felt despair? Have you been unkind to someone who meant you well? Have you been selfish, seeing only your own grief? All of these—and many other aspects of mourning—are opportunities for prayers of confession. First, think about how you have hurt others. Second, acknowledge these wrongs honestly to God, speaking directly to Him. Third, ask God for forgiveness and cleansing. Fourth, accept God's attention and forgiveness. Finally, ask God to help you to avoid these sins as you go forward.

Volunteer. There's no question that any number of individuals and groups need your help. You may not know it, or you may, in the midst of your grief, not be responsive to these needs. But they offer a tremendous opportunity for active prayer. It's good to make the effort to help others even while you mourn; it forces you out of your seclusion, allows you to be of service, and helps you to recognize that you have value separate and apart from your life with the one you've lost.

The type of volunteer experience you choose should be guided by your feelings: If you've lost someone who spent time in a nursing home, hospice, or hospital, it may be too painful to return immediately to that environment. Instead, volunteer to work with children, in a local soup kitchen or food pantry, at the library, or at church. On the other hand, if you are comforted by being in the kind of place your loved one was, volunteering in a hospital or nursing home can be very rewarding.

Before beginning any volunteer program, ask God for the strength to put aside fear and misgiving, the perseverance to follow through on opportunities to be of service, the compassion to understand those who will be served, and the kindness to touch them.

Resume a favorite hobby or habit. Not long ago, a good friend of mine lost her husband of fifty years to a brutally debilitating cancer. The situation was made more difficult by the fact that his disease had probably been caused by his former work environment. For months he was in and out of hospitals, and though his family insisted on keeping him at home for as long as possible, he spent his last hours in a hospice with my friend and their daughters and grandchildren gathered around him. For the whole time he was sick and for a long time afterward, my friend couldn't bring herself to read. Reading had been her favorite pastime; she was on a first-name basis with the local library staff, and she and her husband had spent hours talking about books. But after he died, she couldn't bring herself to read. "I just can't get interested," she told me shortly after he died.

Then one day she told me that she'd checked the latest best-seller list and, seeing new books by two of her favorite authors, she reserved them at the library. "Will you read them when they come in?" I asked. She didn't laugh at my blundering question, but I heard the smile in her voice when she replied, "I hope so."

Returning to the things you've enjoyed in the past can provide you with much-needed normalcy and a healthy routine. Resuming a hobby or favored habit is an act of faith, a way of acknowledging that God is still in His heaven, and life goes on, that joy is part of God's plan for you, even though you may not believe it at the moment. So whether the plan is to check out a good book, prepare a terrific meal, take a class, knit, write a letter to the editor, exercise, go out to lunch, attend church, go antique shopping or plant a garden, first pray for the courage to believe that what has brought you pleasure in the past will eventually do so again. And ask God for the fortitude to keep at it until you begin to enjoy it again.

THANKSGIVING

When you are mourning, it can be very difficult, if not impossible, to think of reasons to give thanks, and so it's helpful to focus on simple things. Here are some suggestions to help you focus on the things you can still be thankful for:

Father, thank You for the rising and the setting of the sun, the appearance of the moon and stars, rhythm of the seasons, and all Your works in the world that let me know that life continues.

Dear Lord, thank You for the kindness I've received from the people in my community and from those who love me.

Merciful Jesus, thank You for weeping at the grave of Lazarus and showing us that, like us, You feel the anguish of loss.

Almighty God, thank You for keeping close to me even when I can't feel or respond to Your presence.

Guiding Light, thank You for sending me advisors, friends, and trusted family members who can help me.

Redeemer, thank You for the gentle oblivion of sleep.

Father, thank You for the release of tears.

Jesus, thank You for rising from death and providing me with hope in my sorrow.

God of the living, thank You for reminding me that You will reunite me with my beloved in Your own time.

PSALM-AS-PRAYER

These verses from Psalm 31 vividly describe the sorrows that beset those who deeply mourn a loved one: the need for refuge, the sense of abandonment, the feeling of being trapped inside a paralyzing maze, the temptation to idolize the deceased, the impression of unwitting rejection by friends and neighbors who fear the proximity of death and grief. If you are mourning, you'll find a spiritual home in this psalm.

PSALM 31:1–12, 14, 16
PRAYER AND PRAISE FOR DELIVERANCE
FROM ENEMIES

In you, O Lord, I seek refuge;
do not let me ever be put to shame;
in your righteousness deliver me.

Incline your ear to me;
rescue me speedily.
Be a rock of refuge for me,
a strong fortress to save me.
You are indeed my rock and my fortress;
for your name's sake lead me and guide me,
take me out of the net that is hidden for me,
for you are my refuge.
Into your hand I commit my spirit;
You have redeemed me, O Lord, faithful God
You hate those who pay regard to worthless idols,
but I trust in the Lord.
I will exult and rejoice in your steadfast love,
because you have seen my affliction;
You have taken heed of my adversities,
and have not delivered me into the hand of the enemy;
You have set my feet in a broad place.
Be gracious to me, O Lord, for I am in distress;
My eye wastes away from grief,
My soul and body also.
For my life is spent with sorrow,
and my years with sighing;
my strength fails because of my misery,
and my bones waste away.
I am the scorn of all my adversaries,
a horror to my neighbors,
an object of dread to my acquaintances;

those who see me in the street flee from me.
I have been passed out of mind like one who is dead;
I have become like a broken vessel.

. . .

But I trust in you, O Lord;
I say, "You are my God."

. . .

Let your face shine upon your servant;
save me in your steadfast love.

SUGGESTED CLOSING PRAYER

Father, my grief has made me mute. I don't know what to say; I feel nothing but sorrow; I can do nothing but weep. And when my tears are spent, my eyes look out on a cold world, dim, dry, lifeless. There are times when I'm not sure You are listening. O Lord, I need Your comfort! Help me to know You are there. Teach me to make my silence a prayer, my sorrow an opening to Your love, my tears a song. Slip Your hand into mine and let my weak grip be strengthened. Most of all, Lord, help me to never lose sight of Your presence, Your love. You've told me it is there for the asking: Lord, I ask.

BIBLE REFERENCE

The daughter of Herodias danced before the company, and she pleased Herod so much that he promised on oath to grant her whatever she might ask. Prompted by her mother, she said, "Give me the head of John the Baptist here on a platter." The king was grieved, yet out of regard for his oath and for the guests, he commanded it to be given; he sent and had John beheaded. . . . Now when Jesus heard this, he withdrew from there in a boat to a deserted place by himself. . . .

—MATTHEW 14:6–10, 13

When You're Troubled by Doubts

WE'VE ALL PROBABLY BEEN surprised by stories about people who appear to have great faith, and yet as it turns out, also experience painful doubt. Sometimes those who devote their lives to loving and studying the Lord are those most plagued by excruciating questions and uncertainties. Mother Teresa's personal papers revealed how she struggled with a lack of faith, a belief that she could not communicate with God, and a deep sense of unworthiness. The Spanish mystic John of the Cross used the now-famous phrase "the dark night of the soul" to describe his wrenching struggles with his feelings of the absence of God. Susannah Wesley, the mother of the founder of Methodism, struggled for years with doubts about her salvation.

If such amazing souls as these experienced doubt and confusion in their faith, what is to become of the rest of us? Perhaps the best way to tackle this question is to say at the outset that there is no shame in doubt. Indeed, some of those who were closest to Jesus were themselves doubters. Peter doubted even after he all but dared Jesus to perform a miracle:

But when the disciples saw him walking on the lake, they were terrified. . . . Peter answered him, "Lord, if it is you, command me to come to you on the water." He said, "Come." So Peter got out of the boat, started walking on the water, and came toward Jesus. But when he noticed the strong wind, he became frightened, and beginning to sink, he cried out, "Lord, save me!" Jesus immediately reached out his hand and caught him, saying to him, "You of little faith, why did you doubt?"

—MATTHEW 14:26–31

And when Jesus most needed him to believe, Peter not only doubted, but also denied:

Now Peter was sitting outside. . . . A servant-girl came to him and said, "You also were with Jesus the Galilean." But he denied it before all of them. . . . When he went out to the porch, another servant-girl saw him, and she said to the bystanders, "This man was with Jesus of Nazareth." Again he denied it. . . . After a little while the bystanders came up and said to Peter, "Certainly you are also one of them, for your accent betrays you." Then he began to curse and he swore an oath, "I do not know the man!" At that moment the cock crowed. Then Peter remembered what Jesus had said: "Before the cock crows, you will deny me three times." And he went out and wept bitterly.

—MATTHEW 26:69–75

Another apostle, Thomas, has gone down in Christian history as the one who doubted Jesus' resurrection. Even today, we call someone who lacks faith in a particular outcome a "doubting Thomas."

> *But Thomas . . . was not with them when Jesus came. So the other disciples told him, "We have seen the Lord." But he said to them, "Unless I see the mark of the nails in his hands, and put my finger in the mark of the nails and my hand in his side, I will not believe." A week later . . . . Jesus came and stood among them and said, "Peace be with you." Then he said to Thomas, "Put your finger here and see my hands. Reach out your hand and put it in my side. Do not doubt but believe."*
>   —JOHN 20:24–27

The apostle Paul had to be blinded and knocked to the ground before he relinquished his doubts about the new church and its message about Jesus:

> *Meanwhile Saul, still breathing threats and murder against the disciples of the Lord. . . . as he was going along and approaching Damascus, suddenly a light from heaven flashed around him. He fell to the ground and heard a voice saying to him, "Saul, Saul, why do you persecute me?" He asked, "Who are you, Lord?" The reply came, "I am Jesus, whom you are persecuting. But get up and enter the city, and you will be told what you*

are to do." The men who were traveling with him stood
speechless because they heard the voice but saw no one.
Saul got up from the ground, and though his eyes were
open, he could see nothing. . . .   —ACTS 9:1–8

So the first lesson of doubt is that if and when we doubt, we are certainly in good company! Even those who experienced Jesus firsthand sometimes felt uncertain and doubtful. The clear and comforting truth about doubt is that there can be no doubt without first having an experience of Jesus. It is only when we have established our faith in God that we can question.

This kind of doubt is very much like a teenager questioning his parents. For twelve years, the child was completely dependent upon the parents. He knew that he needed and loved his parents, and even when they disciplined him, he believed that they loved him. Even when he didn't understand why they did what they did, he had faith that they were acting in his best interest. But when the child grows older, he begins to doubt and question the parents.

What has changed? A number of things: First, after years of trusting his parents and secure in their love, the teenager feels safe questioning them. He knows they will not abandon him just because he is skeptical or even impertinent. In the same way, we are only capable of questioning when we feel safe in God's love and presence.

Second, the boy is becoming a man, and thinks he is able

to understand his parents and their motives. Of course, this is not necessarily true. The adolescent is trying to become *like* his parents, and so he thinks he can make the same kinds of decisions that they can. He believes he's mature and knows enough to question his parents' decisions. Again, the same thing happens to us: The more mature we become in our faith, the more we think we know, the more we think ourselves able to make decisions about faith and the more we find ourselves questioning.

The Jewish people, our parents in faith and those with whom we share the Old Testament, have a long history of discourse and discussion about God. Studying and questioning God's Word is a natural outgrowth of their faith. The Jewish people have reached a comfort level with God through thousands of years of personal interaction and seeking. Time after time we see Jesus entering into these kinds of discussions with His contemporaries as well as with scribes and Pharisees. When He was twelve, His frantic parents found Him in the temple, deep in discussion with the rabbis there. Jesus joined in the Jewish tradition that valued exploring the words and teachings of God. Their questions, their discourse, their millennia of learning about God and the Scriptures have been the foundation of their religion.

In fact, the more you know about God, the more questions you will likely have. This too is only natural. Like the small child, at first we know only that our Heavenly Father loves us, cares for us, and gives us everything we need. That's all we need to know as children. As our faith and our learning about God grows, we come to know more about Him, about what He's done throughout history, what His relationship is with the rest of the world, Who He is separate and apart from our own needs. Suddenly, we want to know even more. We want to understand why He does what He does, and perhaps most pressingly, why He *doesn't* do some things. We have questions! And when we realize we can't know everything—can't even know most things about Him—because of our limited human nature, we become frustrated and unhappy. From those feelings and limitations come the doubts.

While it may not be flattering to consider your doubts as an adolescent response to God, it should be comforting. When you realize that God is too magnificent and glorious to be hurt or offended by your doubts and questions, you can relax and begin to pray to the very One you question. God knows that your doubts are largely an attempt to get closer to Him and understand Him. But to make your doubts useful, to turn each question into a stepping-stone on your faith journey, you must pray with and through doubt. Doubt can become prayer simply because doubt is born of faith.

IDENTIFYING THE SOURCE

You can better "pray your doubt" by first exploring its source. My friend J is one of my "readers," someone I've asked to read my manuscripts before I send them to a publisher. I have a few trusted and insightful friends who do this for me, and their comments and suggestions vastly improve my work. After J read something I wrote about dealing with anxiety through faith, she began talking to me about her own doubts. She wondered why churches that claimed to embody love of God and Jesus would feud about which hymns to sing or which congregant was worthy of being a church leader. She wondered why so much evil was done by people claiming to be acting in God's name. She wondered how she would raise her young daughter in a world so fraught with danger and meanness. And she wondered why God allowed all this.

But she didn't count these questions as impediments to faith. Instead, she used them to strengthen her faith—she turned them into a form of prayer. After acknowledging her questions and doubts, she turned to things in life that taught her about the wonder and glory and love of God. She learned to associate everything beautiful and healthy with God. She came to believe that the spirit of God resided in every good thing and in every good action. When she saw her daughter act generously toward another child, she saw God. When she took in a magnolia tree in full spring bloom, she thought of God. When she read a good book, she thanked God for its author and for the time to read it. When her little girl danced in her blinking light, glow-in-the-dark sneakers, she felt that God was as delighted as she was at her child's joy.

J used her doubt to make her life into one long prayer. She was able to do this because she understood that we don't have to become mired in our doubts. We can acknowledge them, understand that they are a natural outgrowth of our faith, and use them to create prayer opportunities. Her antidote to doubt about why God allowed evil was to look for God in everything good, and in this way she prayed in and through her doubt.

I met a woman named Judy when I started to bring Communion to an older woman in a neighboring town. Because the woman had no family in America, Judy had become her caretaker, confidante, meal provider, laundress, driver, banker and peacemaker. Judy willingly took on the challenging personal commitment that all these roles required. Her dedication was astounding, the more so because she thought it unremarkable. "I just do what I do," she would say, dismissing any and all praise that came her way. As I got to know her, I learned that she had cared for other older people.

One day when I mentioned (again) that I thought she was terrific, she explained that she felt aging and death were natural processes, and she felt that God had given her the gift to be able to help people through these times. "It's not death that bothers me," she said slowly. "It's all the suffering that happens before death. Why does that have to happen? Why can't people just go to sleep?"

I had no answer—who really does? But Judy had not allowed herself to be paralyzed or made helpless by it. Having identified her central question, she made it her work to do everything in her considerable power to ease the very pain and fear she could not understand. What a perfect way to pray her doubt!

Despite his gentle and accepting attitude, when it comes to work my husband Charlie is both competitive and very successful. A colleague once accurately described him as an A-type personality hiding behind a B-type demeanor. From creating, and rowing on, a crew in college to a long career working with and in state government, he dislikes losing and seldom does. Not surprisingly, spirituality hadn't been his strong suit. When we met nine years ago, I was horrified during one of our first romantic dinners when he unwittingly spoiled the atmosphere by telling me that his "faith" consisted of believing that the strong and sometimes brutal are the ones that survive in the animal—and human—world while God simply looks on from afar.

I fled to the ladies' room, and returned only when I'd controlled my urge to start weeping into my poached salmon and wild rice. How would I deal with such a deep, even angry, doubt about God's capacity to love and care for us? Did he really mean it? We didn't talk any more about it that night. But over the next few days, I could think of little else. I couldn't understand how he lived with such a belief. With such a philosophy, how did he avoid giving into cynicism, if not despair? He knew he had distressed me and was not anxious to talk more about the matter, and my questions were to no avail. So I did the only thing someone so deeply in love could do: I waited and I watched. And I began to understand how Charlie "prayed his doubt." It was in how he lived his life.

In observing him carefully, I began to see his exceptional kindness and courtesy in another way. His willingness to help virtually anyone (including some people I might have turned away from, I was ashamed to note) was a prayer that counteracted his belief about the cruelty in life. His capacity to quickly forgive and forget any transgression or insult was a prayer for civility in the world. His generosity was a prayer against selfishness and the desire for financial success at any cost. His sense of justice and his dedication to pursuing it was a prayer that denied the power of oppression.

Gradually I came to understand that his doubt, his sad and mostly accurate perspective on the world, was something he chose to counter in every aspect of his life. Over the years he's come to develop a stronger relationship with God, and now believes that God's goodness can be seen in our world and in his own life. And I'm eternally grateful that I didn't bolt that first night after dinner!

Whatever the source of your doubt, once you name it, you can use that knowledge to pray through it, to find the antidote—if not the precise answers to your questions—within the very faith that allows you to question.

Letting Go

While identifying the source of doubt and learning to pray through doubt is important, it's essential to admit that doubt can sometimes become a dangerous form of arrogance. Let's return to the example of the teenager questioning and even defying his parents. The teenager thinks he knows as much—or more—than his parents. Based on that rather premature and almost always incorrect belief, he questions the decisions of his parents because he absolutely *knows* he could do better. The fact is, a teenager who feels equal or superior to his parents is demonstrating arrogance, though in most cases, it's an immature arrogance based in ignorance and naiveté.

When we think we know enough, have experienced enough, to question God, we are exhibiting some level of childlike pride. Granted, if asked directly, we would probably deny that we think we know better than God. But isn't this what we are truly doing, even if we don't mean to, when we make doubt a way of life? How different are we from the child who defies his parents' decisions because he thinks he knows better?

We saw a lot of this after the attacks of September 11, 2001. It was quite natural for the children of God to question their Father in the face of such a tragedy. "How could God have allowed this?" people cried in anguish. "How could it have happened if God really loved us?" The questions abounded.

What was even more disturbing to me—and much more presumptuous—than the questions people asked about 9/11 were the many explanations people offered, especially those that made the rounds on the Internet. The first, especially in the case of 9/11, was an innocent, agonized seeking; the second was an overbearing, if well-meaning, attempt to speak on behalf of God.

The answers varied. Some suggested that God had been responsible for saving the many people who were *not* killed that day. Others painted a picture of God busily drawing the souls of the murdered to heaven. Another suggested that God was punishing America because He did not like the way some of us live.

The fact is, none of these "answers" really answers the question "Why?" In fact, some of them must have seemed downright cruel to the victims and their families. As we've seen, these kinds of explanations didn't work too well for Job and his friends, and they're not likely to work any better for us now. For who among us can truly know the mind of God? Even with the entirety of the Bible as our study resource, we cannot come close to a full understanding.

The simple, though often difficult to accept, truth is that our questions and doubts must be tempered by humility. Sooner or later, we must be willing to let go of our self-importance, our need for all the answers. We live in a world where science, technology, and the media have led us to believe that all the answers are available and accessible to us, if only we ask the right questions and keep asking them. We've asked questions about disease, and medical science has answered so well that we live longer and healthier lives.

We ask questions about what's going on in nations across the world, and the media provides in-depth coverage and tells us secrets divulged by unnamed sources. We ask questions about what's likely to happen in the future, and a multitude of pundits, scholars, foundations and government agencies spew out relevant data, studies, predictions and polls.

It's in our nature to question, particularly in the face of personal or communal tragedy. We are, after all, only human, and God knows that—often better than we do! He does not reject us for questioning or doubting, just as no good parent will abandon a child who questions or even defies him. Where we run into trouble in our relationship with God and in our prayer is when we demand answers, or worse, try to provide them for God. And even then, the trouble is of our own making, not of God's. When we allow our doubts, our pressing need for answers, to overwhelm our prayer and our faith, we hurt only ourselves. God is hurt only in that He is always hurt when we injure ourselves. Our presumption is transformed from naive questioning to willful arrogance.

Practicing humility, then, is another essential way to pray through doubt. Remember that Jesus said, "For all who exalt themselves will be humbled, and those who humble themselves will be exalted" (Luke 14:11). And,

> *Jesus called for [the children] and said, "Let the little children come to me, and do not stop them; for it is to such as these that the kingdom of God belongs. Truly I*

tell you, whoever does not receive the kingdom of God
as a little child will never enter it."

—LUKE 18:16–17

If doubts and the demand for answers are crippling your relationship with God and your prayer life, try praying the following prayer:

All-knowing Father, I have paralyzed myself with doubt.
I have silenced my prayers with questions.
I have separated myself from you with my incessant need
for answers.
I have injured myself, Lord.
And yet, even knowing the damage I have done, I cannot
seem to walk away from my questions and doubts.
Help me, Lord, to let go of my arrogance, my belief that I
deserve an answer, just because I want one.
Help me to realize that my human mind is incapable
of grasping You, of understanding the complexity
of Your answers.
Even if You fed them to me a little at a time, even if You gave
me just a word a day, it would be too much for me.
Remind me that Your caressing whisper is all I can handle,
and teach me to yearn for that gentle sound.
Help me to be humble as the Israelites were humble in the
desert when they fled from the magnificence of Your face lest
they die at the very sight of such wonder.

Teach me to act always like Your child,
to cry out in need and want,
and to trust that You will give me what I need, what I can
handle, and not necessarily what I think I want.
Lord, protect me from those false prophets who Jesus
warned us would claim to speak in Your name
and thus try to deceive us.
In my newfound humility, let me seek Your love,
not demand Your answers.
Let me seek the calm of Your presence, not the clamor
of false explanations.
Let me seek the courage that comes with Your strength,
not make a virtue of my weakness.
Let me seek to "pray my doubt," and not let my doubt
divide me from You.
Let me surrender my presumption, and in so doing,
surrender to You.
Let me do as Jesus instructed,
and become like a little child in my prayer
and my dependence upon You.

PRAYING WITH THOMAS AND PETER

We've already looked at some of the Scriptures that describe the doubts of Thomas and Peter. Though Thomas is famous for doubting Jesus' Resurrection, Peter, Jesus' choice to lead the church, was also sometimes a doubter, as evidenced by his constant questioning of Christ. Yet the two apostles were very different in *how* they doubted.

Thomas doubted as a result of significant tragedies that directly affected him. We first see him doubting when Jesus announces that He will return to Bethany only after His good friend Lazarus has died.

> *Then after this he said to the disciples, "Let us go to Judea again." The disciples said to him, "Rabbi, the Jews were just now trying to stone you, and are you going there again?" . . . Then Jesus told them plainly, "Lazarus is dead. For your sake I am glad I was not there, so that you may believe. But let us go to him." Thomas, who was called the Twin, said to his fellow disciples, "Let us also go, that we may die with him."*
> —JOHN 11:7–8, 14–16

Thomas was responding to the dual crises of Lazarus' death and Jesus' imminent arrest. He later doubts again as a result of the multiple shocks associated with Jesus' trial and crucifixion. These were devastating events to Thomas, a cautious man who'd given up everything to follow Jesus. In these terrifying occurrences, Thomas sees his world crumbling, so he doubts.

Peter, on the other hand, is an everyday sort of pessimistic doubter.

From that time on, Jesus began to show his disciples that
he must go to Jerusalem and undergo great suffering at
the hands of the elders and chief priests and scribes, and
be killed, and on the third day be raised. And Peter took
him aside and began to rebuke him, saying, "God forbid
it, Lord! This must never happen to you."

—MATTHEW 16:21–22

Later, we see Peter doubting even Jesus' financial decisions, and so the apostle goes so far as to lie for Jesus!

The collectors of the temple tax came to Peter and said,
"Does your teacher not pay the temple tax?" He said,
"Yes, he does."...   —MATTHEW 17:24–25

Jesus, knowing what Peter has done, makes him an honest
man while also instructing him:

"So that we do not give offense to them, go to the lake
and cast a hook; take the first fish that comes up; and
when you open its mouth, you will find a coin; take
that and give it to them for you and me."

—MATTHEW 17:26–27

And, of course, Peter is the only one who dares to question Jesus about the potential rewards for the disciples.

Then Peter said in reply, "Look, we have left everything
and followed you. What then will we have?"

—MATTHEW 19:27

Even at the Last Supper, Peter continues to defy Jesus, resisting when Jesus attempts to wash the apostles' feet.

> *[Jesus] came to Simon Peter, who said to him, "Lord are you going to wash my feet?" Jesus answered, "You do not know now what I am doing, but later you will understand." Peter said to him, "You will never wash my feet."*   —JOHN 13:6–8

And even after Jesus has risen and is forgiving Peter for his denials, Peter *still* becomes impatient with Jesus.

> *Jesus said to Simon Peter, "Simon son of John, do you love me more than these?" He said to him, "Yes, Lord; you know that I love you." Jesus said to him, "Feed my lambs." A second time he said to him, "Simon son of John, do you love me?" He said to him, "Yes, Lord; you know that I love you." Jesus said to him, "Tend my sheep." He said to him the third time, "Simon son of John, do you love me?" Peter felt hurt because he said to him the third time, "Do you love me?" And he said to him, "Lord, you know everything; you know that I love you." . . . Peter turned and saw the disciple whom Jesus loved following them. . . . When Peter saw him, he said to Jesus, "Lord, what about him?" Jesus said to him, "If it is my will that he remain until I come, what is that to you? Follow me!"*   —JOHN 21:15–17, 20–22*

These are just a few of the instances in which Peter questions Jesus, and though it may seem to us that he is constantly putting his foot in his mouth, this is simply who Peter is and how he communicates his anxieties. Peter's doubts are habitual, not provoked by a specific, life-altering, personal event as is the case with Thomas. It's worth noting that Jesus, fully knowing the leadership role He intended for Peter, accepts Peter's questions and invariably uses them as occasions to teach His apostle. So while Thomas questions Jesus in large crises, Peter questions Jesus in everyday matters. Most of us fall into one—and sometimes both—of those categories. Some of us doubt when terrible things happen to us or those we love; others of us doubt because day-to-day life can be so full of uncertainties. In whichever way your doubts manifest themselves, you can look for help to the apostle whose doubting "style" most resembles your own.

If your doubts are the result of a personal tragedy or disaster, you can study how the pensive apostle Thomas overcame his uncertainty. Thomas was a model of patience. He always waited for Jesus to dissipate his doubts. When he questioned Jesus' decision to return to Bethany after Lazarus' death, Thomas didn't rage against Jesus; he didn't demand an answer; he didn't give up his discipleship even though he was about to put himself in serious danger as an associate of Jesus; he didn't try to protect himself by refusing to go to Bethany. Indeed, he was the first to say—albeit with a clear despairing accent—that they must go with Jesus into the lion's den. And what was the result of Thomas' loyal waiting in the face of such anxiety? He witnessed a miracle like no other, his Lord's raising of a dead man. Talk about an antidote to doubt!

You can also identify with Thomas' fallibility when just a short time later, he is again plagued by doubt despite what he has already seen. And again, Thomas' doubt is a result of a terrible disaster: He has witnessed his Lord and Master's betrayal, humiliation, abandonment and brutal political murder. Thomas, being Thomas, is again overcome with doubt when his fellow disciples tell him that Jesus is risen. How can he, traumatized and afraid, even begin to believe such a thing?

What does Thomas do? He could flee, leaving the danger of Jerusalem behind him. But he doesn't. He could join the bandwagon of those who betrayed Jesus to keep themselves safe. But he doesn't. He could urge the followers of Jesus to join the powerful rebel Zealots and exact vengeance for Jesus' murder. But he doesn't. Thomas waits on the Lord. And when the Lord shows up, dispelling all of Thomas' doubts forever, Thomas is ready to fall on his knees in adulation.

Can you even begin to imagine the impact of these two miracles on Thomas? You should try, because they can have the same impact on you when you struggle with doubt born of your own fears and tragedies. Thomas' prayer was to be still and wait. This kind of waiting is a way of telling God, "I don't have the answers but I know You do, and I know that You will not abandon me." It was a form of praying Thomas had to return to frequently during his time with Jesus. It's a form of praying that can help you today with your own crisis-based doubts.

Several years ago, a friend of mine had an experience that fit well into the "Thomas style." His twin sister died unexpectedly after a short and seemingly mild illness. He was devastated. He and his sister had been very close, and he blamed himself for her miserable life. She had been married for years to an abusive man, and there had been nothing our friend could do about it. Now he felt a combination of grief and guilt for what he had not been able to do on her behalf. Though he had what he calls a "Sunday sort of religion," his faith was not particularly strong. When his sister died, he began questioning why her life had been so hard. Why had God allowed it? Why had God not pushed him into helping her? How could she be at peace?

"The night of her wake," my friend recalls, "I came close to having a nervous breakdown. My friends were worried that the next day they'd be carrying the casket down the church aisle and then carrying me out the church door on a stretcher. I didn't disagree with them. I went home that night and just lay down, knowing I would never sleep. All I could do was wait. And while I waited for the dawn, this amazing feeling came over me. It was peace. It was a sense that my sister was at peace; that I was forgiven; that she was completely okay. I know it sounds strange, but I felt a kind of joy. I knew God was with me, and that He was with her. I slept. The next day at the funeral, my friends were prepared for the worst. They couldn't believe the transformation." My friend had followed the same path as Thomas: crisis, doubt, acknowledgment, waiting, grace.

To overcome the kind of crisis of doubt that is embodied in Thomas' story, you can pray:

Jesus, Lord, my sorrow and fear has overtaken me.
I don't know which way to look, what to think, where to turn.
When I consider my life right now, doubts and
concerns crowd my mind.
The prayers I've prayed before seem inadequate now.
And yet I know You are present, Lord, just as Thomas knew
that You were present and powerful even when he couldn't
understand Your words and actions.
Teach me to wait upon You, Jesus, as You taught
Thomas to wait.
Grant me the patience to wait through this time
of chaos and distress.
Thomas waited even when he couldn't see or hear You.
Even when hope abandoned him, he waited.
Help me to wait in silence when I can't see or hear You, Lord.

Even when hope abandons me, let me wait,
and let my waiting be a prayer.
As You did with Thomas, dearest Lord, turn my sorrow
and confusion to joy!
And when You offer me understanding,
grant me the grace to embrace Your gift.

If you doubt the way Peter doubted, if the increasingly complex events of daily life stymie and disturb you, think of Peter. No matter how often Peter questioned the Lord, he always brought his concerns directly to Jesus. He never hid them or tried to figure them out on his own. At one point, puzzled over Jesus' teaching on forgiveness, Peter questioned Him directly, asking for specifics.

> *Then Peter came up and said to him, "Lord, how often*
> *shall my brother sin against me, and I forgive him? As*
> *many as seven times?" Jesus said to him, "I do not say*
> *to you seven times, but seventy times seven."*
>
> —MATTHEW 18:21–22 (RSV)

It's vital to acknowledge Peter's dogged willingness to bring his questions and doubts directly to Jesus, because if you don't follow his example, you might find yourself suffocated by an avalanche of small and large doubts. If you don't bring them to the Lord as they come to you, they can pile up, adding dead weight to your prayers and faith. Peter never worried about whether he was pestering Jesus; it never occurred to the bold apostle that Jesus wouldn't want to be bothered with him! Nor should you worry about offending the Lord or asking for His help.

I am always dismayed when I hear people say, "Oh, God can't be bothered with my little problems; He has enough big things to concentrate on!" As if God can't "concentrate" on more than one thing! Of course God wants to hear from us! Of course He wants us to lay our sorrows, worries, questions at His feet! Does He need to hear from us in order to know our thoughts? No. He knows everything, including everything about each of us, but that's not the point in bringing our thoughts and concerns to Him. Beseeching the Lord for help and understanding—as Peter did continually for three whole years—is a healthy exercise for us. Bringing ourselves and our distress before the Lord as Peter did is the perfect way to pray about, and through, doubt.

My uncertainties tend to be in the Peter style. Though I've been stunned by crises in my life and in the lives of those around me, these big events do not usually shake my faith. It's the little things, the nagging questions that occur every day, that drag on my faith. Simply put, I'm a worrier, and I've had to admit to myself that my daily anxieties can lead to doubt if I don't pay attention. I even worry that my worrying might offend the Lord! So Peter comes in handy when I want to gain some perspective, particularly on how much God loves and forgives me—as often as I need it!

Another lesson Peter provides for me is that he never

hesitated to bring his questions and doubts to Jesus. No one could ever accuse Peter of holding back! So I'm learning that rather than cower in the shadows with my worries and questions, I can—and should—bring them directly to Jesus just as Peter did. My questions, then, become a form of prayer, and I bring them to God as a gift, acknowledging that I just don't have all the answers. Asked in this way, as prayer, my questions become an admission of my ignorance and incapacity to comprehend the deeper mysteries of God. I try to think of them as my way of laying myself open before God and admitting that I need His help in understanding what He wants and in knowing how I can become closer to Him.

Peter has also taught me that no matter how often I bring my concerns before the Lord, I may not always get the answers I most desire. No doubt Peter didn't always get the response he wanted from Jesus, but Peter was never shy, and he always went back for more even after he'd received an answer that didn't please him. It seems pretty clear that when Peter asked Jesus how often he must forgive—and even fool-ishly suggests that he knows the answer is seven times (how, Peter implies in his question, could it be *more* than that?)— he was not expecting to be told seventy times seven! We can imagine Peter wincing, considering arguing with Jesus, and then finally accepting the Lord's Word and wandering off to ponder it . . . until he came up with a new worry or doubt.

Peter is a terrific model for me in many ways. When I have my own questions about how forgiving I'm supposed to be, I'm forced to look at the answer Jesus gave the curious fisherman, no matter how hard it may seem to me at the time. And when I'm ready to fall under the burden of the many daily questions that result from my habitual worry, I am relieved to remember Jesus' last words to his most faithful apostle: "If it is my will . . . what is that to you? Follow me!" (John 21:22).

Finally, in Peter I am blessed to be reminded that Jesus must indeed have been pleased with the incessant questioning of the blustering apostle. In the end, Jesus rewarded Peter's devotion and dedication to learning His will by making a fisherman the leader of the apostles. The Lord wants me to seek Him and His will; my doubts and questions can be transformed into that kind of holy yearning. And perhaps the most important question that passed between Jesus and Peter was the one that Jesus asked Peter:

> *[Jesus] said to them, "But who do you say that I am?" Simon Peter answered, "You are the Messiah, the Son of the living God." And Jesus answered him, "Blessed are you, Simon son of Jonah! For flesh and blood has not revealed this to you, but my Father in heaven. And I tell you, you are Peter, and on this rock I will build my church. . . ."* —MATTHEW 16:15–18

What better proof have we that it is not a matter of *whether* we doubt or question, it is a matter of *how* we do it. Peter did it with love in his heart and yearning in his spirit. We should do the same.

To address the daily or habitual doubt that you may share with Peter, you can pray:

Beloved Lord, You know me better than anyone,
better, even, than I know myself.
You know that my mind is often consumed with worry.
I am anxious about so many things in my life, in the lives of
those around me, and in the state of the world.
Lord, forgive me when I allow these concerns
to threaten my faith.
Help me to model myself after Your intrepid apostle Peter.
You chose Peter to be Your rock in spite of—or because of—
his many questions.
Peter asked them with a heart full of love and a spirit
that sought only You.
Help me also to turn my questions, my doubts, my worries
into a seeking prayer.
Let me ask my questions out of an earnest desire to grow
closer to You, to become more fully Your child.
Diminish any negative or paralyzing power doubt holds over
me, Lord, by drawing me to You.
Remind me that You do have all the answers, even if I am too

limited to understand them, too stubborn to accept them, too
frightened to make the changes they may require of me.
Teach me to lay my concerns and questions at Your feet, Lord.
Let them be my offering to You, a demonstration of my need
and desire for You.
Allow me to leave them there, to let them go, to embrace Your
summons to Peter: "Follow me!"

THANKSGIVING

If you are struggling with doubt, a simple prayer of thanks can be a powerful antidote. In the act of giving thanks, you acknowledge God's power and presence in the world. Prayers like these can give you an uncomplicated way to recognize the Lord. As always, feel free to adapt them according to your needs.

Forgiving Father, thank You for the moon glimmering on the water, for the sun playing on the fields and for every sign of Your marvelous work in nature.

Jesus, thank You for showing us in Your relationship with Your disciples, particularly Peter, that You understand and forgive our doubt.

Lord, my Protector, thank You for coming among us as a man Who was subject to the same temptations and doubts that I experience.

God, thank You for the clear evidence of Your power and Your love in the Bible.

Lord, thank You for renewing Your covenant with humankind again and again and again, for showing me that as long as I come back to You, You will welcome me.

PSALM-AS-PRAYER

In these verses from Psalm 10, the psalmist first warns against paying attention to your doubts or to those who would draw you away from God, then urges you to remember that God is the great Protector of the orphan, the Savior of those in need, and finally encourages you to depend on the Lord for justice and strength.

PSALM 10:1–4, 12–14, 16–18
PRAYER FOR DELIVERANCE FROM ENEMIES

Why, O Lord, do you stand far off?
Why do you hide yourself in times of trouble?
In arrogance the wicked persecute the poor—
let them be caught in the schemes they have devised.
For the wicked boast of the desires of their heart,
those greedy for gain curse and renounce the Lord.
In the pride of their countenance the wicked say,
"God will not seek it out";
all their thoughts are, "There is no God."

. . .

Rise up, O Lord; O God lift up your hand;
do not forget the oppressed.
Why do the wicked renounce God,
and say in their hearts, "You will not call us to account"?
But you do see!
Indeed you note trouble and grief,
that you may take it into your hands;
the helpless commit themselves to you;
You have been the helper of the orphan.

. . .

The Lord is king forever and ever;
the nations shall perish from his land.
O Lord, you will hear the desire of the meek;
you will strengthen their heart,
You will incline your ear to do justice for the orphan
and the oppressed,
so that those from earth may strike terror no more.

SUGGESTED CLOSING PRAYER

Father, sometimes it seems that the more I try to be close to You, the harder it gets! I am troubled by so many questions. There is so much about You that I just don't understand. I want to see Your hand in everything that happens in the world, but I can't.

Lord, help me to realize that I need not understand everything about You, that in fact, no human can. Help me to accept my limitations and to put my seeking to good use. Let my thirst for answers be quenched by Your majesty. And let my efforts to know You better be satisfied by faith.

BIBLE REFERENCE

Jesus cried out with a loud voice, "Eloi, Eloi, lema sabachthani?" which means, "My God, my God, why have you forsaken me?"   —MARK 15:34

When You're Angry and Fearful

THE RAGING FIRES of anger and the icy tentacles of fear can frustrate even the most determined effort to pray. These emotions can take control of the body, mind and spirit, causing everything from serious illness to broken relationships. Fear and anger are closely related, with the former often causing the latter. While some people think of fear as a weakness or vulnerability and anger as a form of strength, anger rarely exists without fear as its nagging catalyst. And our innermost fears often deceive us. Just as we may not be able to discover the origin of a fear, we also may not be able to trace the path fear takes in becoming anger.

PRAYING FOR ENEMIES

When anger and hate fill our lives and minds and hearts, we most need to pray. We also may find that prayer is the farthest thing from our minds, almost inconceivable. How do we pray when our hearts are so darkened? The best answer I've heard to this question came from a missionary I saw late one night on a religious television station. He acknowledged right up front that he was not the easiest person to get along with, and in fact, that he was something of a grump. He had always struggled with Jesus' admonition to love one's enemies and do good to those who hurt and anger us. Eventually, he said, he tried something that was very simple . . . and very difficult. He started to pray for people he considered his enemies, people he disliked, even, he admitted, people he hated.

"You know," he observed, "over time, I discovered something: It's impossible to hate someone you're praying for. You may still disagree with him. You may still dislike her. You may still avoid spending time with him. You may still argue with her. But if you pray for someone regularly, over the long run your hatred and anger will disappear."

At first, I dismissed the missionary's words as so much "preaching." How could I possibly pray for someone who had caused me so much pain and anger? It required a lot of discipline, but I tried it, and the results surprised me.

The process is very simple. First, just add the name of the person you're angry with to the names of those you pray for daily. At first it may not be possible to do more than mention the person's name. If so, do only that. Simply include him or her by name in your prayers. Don't expect to be instantly filled with forgiveness or loving-kindness, though if that happens, give thanks for it. If you're like me, it will take a while. But you should try to offer these prayers ungrudg-

ingly, leaving out your negative feelings. If you have trouble
with this, ask Jesus to put His words about loving our enemies in your heart as you try again.

Gradually, you can begin to pray more fully for the
person and his or her family and friends. If you don't know
much about them, just pray for them in general; if you do
know them, silently picture them as you offer their names.
As time goes on, add a prayer that God will open their hearts
and yours, that He will touch each in the way that is most
needed. As these prayers are repeated, I've found, it becomes
nearly impossible to continue despising the person or people
you're praying about. Almost without realizing it—and
probably without choosing it—you'll begin to have a stake in
the welfare of your enemies because you are praying for their
welfare every day! This is transforming prayer, and as you
find your feelings changing, go where God leads you, knowing that it may be into a new and different relationship with
your former enemies.

The fear/anger response, whether it affects one or two
people, a country or the world, is closely related to power, or
more precisely, the perceived lack of it. When we feel power-
less, or when we think someone is trying to take our power
from us or assume power over us, we often react with fear
and anger. For many of us, this is practically an automatic
response. Fortunately, most of us are able to stop well short
of letting our violent emotions control us to the point where
we would do physical harm to another. And yet without faith

and prayer, who can say where our most desperate emotions might lead us?

DAVID AND THE MUSIC OF PRAYER

Saul, the first king of Israel, is a perfect example of how fear and anger can turn someone away from prayer and from God. Because he is overshadowed by his successor David, it is easy to forget that Saul was also specially chosen and sanctified by the Lord. From his youth and well into his reign as king of Israel, Saul was upheld by God and God's prophets. Saul even looked the part of one favored by God long before he imagined himself in such a role:

> *There was a man of Benjamin . . . . [who] had a son whose name was Saul, a handsome young man. There was not a man among the people of Israel more handsome than he; he stood head and shoulders above everyone else.* —1 SAMUEL 9:1–2

The young Saul was far from the fearful, jealous king he would become. At first he was too humble to accept the mantle prepared for him, and the prophet Samuel had to persuade him of God's will.

> *Now the day before Saul came, the Lord had revealed to Samuel: "Tomorrow about this time I will send to you a man from the land of Benjamin, and you shall anoint him to be ruler over my people . . . . from the*

hand of the Philistines; for I have seen the suffering of
my people, because their outcry has come to me." When
Samuel saw Saul, the Lord told him, "Here is the man
of whom I spoke to you. He it is who shall rule over my
people." Then Saul approached Samuel inside the gate,
and said, "Tell me, please where is the house of the
seer?" Samuel answered Saul, "I am the seer . . . . And
on whom is all Israel's desire fixed, if not on you and on
all your ancestral house?" Saul answered, "I am only a
Benjaminite, from the least of the tribes of Israel, and
my family is the humblest of all the families of the tribe
of Benjamin. Why then have you spoken to me in this
way?"   —1 SAMUEL 9:15–21

Long after Samuel revealed to Saul that he had been
chosen by God to be the king of the Israelites, Saul could not
bring himself to tell his family. He was still too reticent, too
astonished at this turn of events, even after Samuel had
anointed him and Saul had suddenly begun to prophesy
among a band of prophets as Samuel had predicted. Indeed,
Saul actually went so far as to hide from his people on the
day he was to be proclaimed king.

But when they sought him, he could not be found. So
they inquired again of the Lord, "Did the man come
here?" and the Lord said, "See, he has hidden himself
among the baggage." Then they ran and brought him
from there. . . .   —1 SAMUEL 10:21–23

What happened to this shy, humble young man who went on to become—at least for a while—a strong and wise king? Fear and anger, combined in a heart-twisting form of jealousy, are what happened to Saul. The longer he was king, the more he feared losing the power and control he'd initially rejected but gradually came to prize above all else. With increasing success in battle and domestic affairs, Saul forgot that he owed everything to God. He forgot the young man who was so unassuming and innocent that he could barely accept these gifts. The mature Saul, the increasingly burdened and arrogant king, found himself surrounded by riches. He needed only utter his desire to have it met. He commanded armies of men who would die for him without question. He subdued entire nations that threatened or warred against Israel. Then, just as Saul was becoming all too comfortable with his success, power and control, David came on the scene.

By the time the young shepherd, the youngest son in an undistinguished and most definitely not royal family, began to come to Saul's attention, fear and insecurity had replaced the king's faith in many situations. Restless, harassed by his failures, plagued by nightmares, Saul slipped farther away from God.

David, on the other hand, proved himself skilled in prayer even as a youth. And while Saul's fear and anger prevented him from praying, David used both words and music to pray to God. It was David's music of prayer that soothed

Saul in the king's darkest moments, and it was David's prayer that could—temporarily, at least—banish Saul's distress.

> *Saul sent to Jesse [David's father], saying, "Let David remain in my service, for he has found favor in my sight."* . . . *David took the lyre and played it with his hand, and Saul would be relieved and feel better, and the evil spirit would depart from him.*
>
> —1 SAMUEL 16:22–23

Saul's love for David and David's ability to serve him were soon threatened by the spirit of fearful anger that tore at Saul's soul. When Saul discovered that David was in fact a wise, young warrior who'd replaced Saul in the affection of God and the people of Israel, Saul became furious. And yet Saul still yearned for the relationship he'd had with God before envy and the desire for power had overwhelmed him. This conflict was played out in Saul's relationship with David. Again and again Saul's jealousy and fear compelled him to seek to kill David, and again and again, David's faithfulness touched Saul's withered heart. Even in the midst of his rage and his fear of losing power over himself and his kingdom, Saul saw that David had remained close to the Lord.

> *So David and Abishai went to the army by night; there Saul lay sleeping within the encampment, with his spear stuck in the ground at his head . . . . So David took the spear that was at Saul's head and the water jar, and they went away. No one saw it or knew it, nor did*

anyone awake . . . . Then David went over to the other
side, and stood on top of a hill far away with a great dis-
tance between them. David called to the army . . . . "See
now, where is the king's spear, or the water jar that was
at his head?" Saul recognized David's voice, and said,
"Is that your voice, my son David?" David said, "It is
my voice, my lord, O king." . . . Then Saul said, "I have
done wrong; come back, my son David, for I will never
harm you again, because my life was precious in your
sight today . . . . Blessed be you, my son David!" . . .

—1 SAMUEL 26:7, 12–14, 16–17, 21, 25

Prayer as music played an integral part in David's life, extending far beyond his early practice of playing music in the presence of Saul. Scripture records his laments and pleas for mercy, and songs of triumph and of praise, both in the Books of Samuel and the Bible's own treasury of prayer, the Book of Psalms.

Nor was David ever ashamed to sing and dance before the Lord as we see when he returned the ark of the Lord to Jerusalem.

David danced before the Lord with all his might . . .
with shouting, and with the sound of the trumpet. As
the ark of the Lord came into the city of David, Michal
daughter of Saul looked out of the window, and saw
King David leaping and dancing before the Lord; and
she despised him . . . . David said to Michal, "It was

before the Lord . . . that I have danced. . . . I will make myself yet more contemptible than this, and I will be abased in my own eyes . . . ."   —2 SAMUEL 6:14–16, 21–22

In this passage, we see the reason that David, though he was challenged, tempted and even fell into sin in the course of his long reign, never allowed his anger and fear to separate him from God as Saul had—and as we too often do. David understood that no one except God could truly give him power, nor could he obtain it for himself; and that therefore, no one except God could take power away from him; Michal's scorn cannot touch her husband, the king.

MUSIC AS PRAYER

If you find your own fear and anger to be obstacles to prayer and peace, it is worth noting that David's music was itself a form of prayer, accepted and cherished by God. The phrase, "music hath charms to soothe the savage breast," might well have been applied to David and Saul; and throughout history people have used music not only to praise God but also to seek relief from the fear, sorrow and anger of their lives. The American spiritual came to us from slaves singing and making music to express a combination of distress, anger, fear and hope. Enter a church, no matter how poorly or richly appointed, on any Sunday morning where hymns are sung and played and observe the calming and rejuvenating effects of the music.

I recently saw firsthand the astonishing power of music as prayer. I was visiting a dear friend who had just had a devastating stroke. She was a woman of great elegance and dignity who "kept her own counsel" and who spoke volumes of wisdom through her silence. She seldom spoke about herself in the prayer/discussion group we both attended, but her very presence was a comfort to many of the group's members. I walked somberly into the hospital thinking that if it was hard for me to reflect on how what had happened would affect her, it would have to be crushing, if not impossible, for her. I had even hesitated to visit, knowing that she might not want anyone to see her disabled and unlike herself. I hadn't even told the members of our group, fearing that she would be upset by their visits.

As it turned out, she was happy to see me, managing what her daughters told me was her first smile in some time. But her happiness was short-lived. She was afraid, angry, frustrated and deeply sad. She couldn't speak, but her expressions were nonetheless eloquent, bespeaking her fury and anguish. She had no patience with anything; whenever I tried to engage her, she just turned away.

Except when we sang. On one particularly difficult evening, I took the advice of one of her daughters, and began to sing hymns. I don't have a very good singing voice, but as I began to stutter out the words to "Amazing Grace," her face relaxed and her darting eyes closed gently. She breathed deeply, and then, to my astonishment, she opened her mouth and began to croon the melody of the hymn. She was not yet able to pronounce the words, but her harmonizing was perfect, beautiful, extraordinary. In fact, when I wobbled out of tune, she laughed and shook her head at me. From "Amazing Grace" we moved on to "Go Tell It on the Mountain" and a number of Christmas carols. And they sounded absolutely right on that warm spring night.

That visit with my friend taught me that music is an almost perfect way to pray when spoken prayer is, or seems, out of reach. While my friend was physically unable to speak the words of prayer, if you are struggling with fear and anger, you may also find it impossible to find the words of prayer. In either case, music can be prayer for you, and you have a variety of options. You can participate in musical programs at church or even join the choir. You can sing or play music with friends. You can watch and listen to prayerful music on television or radio. You can attend concerts of gospel, spiritual, Christian or classical music.

You can also play recordings of sacred music in your own home. Depending on your preferences, you can try the sacred works of Bach or Handel, the classic hymns of John and Charles Wesley or Isaac Watts or the great gospel songs of the Brooklyn Tabernacle Choir or Mahalia Jackson. There is also a growing number of Christian musicians who are creating prayerful music relevant to modern times that can be enjoyed by young and old alike. And, as I discovered with my friend, Christmas songs include some of the most inspiring and reverent music ever composed and performed—for any time of the year.

SEEKING CLARITY

Much was made toward the end of the twentieth century about the importance of "getting anger out." During the sixties, seventies and eighties, it became popular to talk about "expressing anger," "venting" and even "blowing off steam" as positive behaviors that would make us healthier as individuals and as a society. The proponents of expressing anger, or "letting it all hang out," suggested that once the poison of fear and its resulting anger was "out there," it would eventually dissipate. And for those who suffered from illnesses related to repressed anxiety and anger, this was not a bad notion. It could be helpful for those who suffered from ulcers or migraines because they had no way to express their fear and anger to find a way to release it. Nor could it be anything but positive for society as a whole to be more honest and open, and less corrupted, by secret resentments and agendas.

That was the theory, at least. As it turned out, just letting out anger was not such a great thing. Expressing anger in the pursuit of physical and emotional health, and the healing of a family, marriage or community is one thing—and for the most part a positive thing. However, the undirected venting of anger is another thing altogether: It simply spawns more fear and rage. Undirected, unproductive anger hasn't led to the resolution of conflict; rather, it has resulted in increased

violence, a lack of civility in public office and private rela-
tions, discourtesy, and heightened stress. Witness our growing attention to newly named behaviors like "road rage" and
the disintegration of polite language and simple courtesy.

I was catching up with a close friend a few weeks ago, and
as always, our talk turned to the joys and woes of family life.
My friend told me about a recent extended-family picnic
that went awry when an in-law decided to voice his many
disappointments with individual relatives and the family in
general. She sighed, shook her head, and said, "You know,
when I was younger, I was all for expressing feelings, airing
things out, being truthful. Maybe the consequences didn't
seem quite so severe then or maybe it's just that I have kids
myself now, but whatever the reason, I've changed my mind.
I mean, is all this bone-jarring honesty really necessary? Do
we really need to hear every complaint and accusation? What
does it accomplish?"

My friend is not the only one asking such questions.
More recently, we've heard more about the ill effects of
unfettered expressions of anger. Now we hear about "anger
management," while convicted criminals, domestic abusers
and even minor offenders are sentenced to programs
designed to help them manage or curb their violent emotions. More and more we are realizing as a society that anger,
unmanaged and unharnessed, with no path to resolution,
can have devastating effects on individuals, families, communities and whole nations.

So what should you do when you find yourself in the

grip of fear and anger? If releasing it like steam from a broken pipe will burn you and those around you, how should you deal with it? This is where active prayer can come in. There are steps you can take to confront your own anger and address it in the context of the situation that is causing it. By deciding to take faithful action to relieve the negative pressure of fear and anger, you are opening the lines of communication to God. It is a way of saying to God, "I recognize that my anxiety and anger are keeping me from You and from those You've put in my life, and I need to do something about that."

The next step in your anger-reduction plan is to ask God to guide the process. This is simply a matter of saying, "Lord, I am committed to changing, to addressing my fear and anger in a way that will lead to resolution and a deeper faith. But I know this won't be easy for me. Please bless my efforts, Father, and stay close to me as I move forward. Help me to feel your presence every step of the way, particularly when I stumble."

Change is never easy. Harriet Lerner, PhD, was one of the first experts to suggest that the unmitigated expression of rage was not only *not* always positive, but positively dangerous and counteractive to resolving the issues that caused the anger. Her 1985 book, *The Dance of Anger*, became an instant best seller. In the book, Dr. Lerner sets out some practical steps for addressing anger. Many of the things she suggests, when used in a faithful, God-centered way, can become active prayer.

Dr. Lerner urges us to break what can seem like an endless

cycle of anger by clarifying the reasons for our anger; learning to communicate our needs and feelings clearly and calmly; acknowledging that we can only change ourselves (no matter how much we think the other person needs to change!); determining how to react to angering situations by changing our usual response and thus breaking the destructive pattern that anger has followed in the past; and maintaining our new attitude and actions when those around us continue the old behavior and resist changing the negative pattern.

Dr. Lerner does not pretend that such behavioral changes will be easy. Often making such alterations in our behavior feels bad before it feels good, and we may feel uncomfortable, wrong, guilty and uncertain as we move to break the negative hold of anger in our lives.

If you want to apply Dr. Lerner's suggestions in a practical and prayerful way, you can take them step-by-step:

1. Clarify the reasons for your anger. PRAY: *Father, help me as I examine myself honestly to discern the reasons for my anger. Guide me to the truth and help me to accept it. Lead me to those individuals and professionals who might help me learn the truth about myself so that I can make the changes needed to help me stay close to You and to improve my life and my attitude.*

2. Learn to communicate your needs and feelings clearly and calmly. PRAY: *Jesus, You were the Master of communication. Even when people didn't want to hear what You had*

to say, You managed to say it in a way that they could not help but attend to. Help me to communicate my thoughts and my needs in a clear, concise manner. Teach me to speak up calmly even in the face of opposition or derision, and to hold my ground without becoming obnoxious, sarcastic or aggressive. Encourage me along this path, so that I never forget that this is the journey to resolution and a more peaceful life.

3. Acknowledge that you can only change yourself. PRAY: *Lord, help me to remember that I cannot change others, I can change only my own behavior. Do not allow me to become discouraged or downhearted if others refuse to change. You continue to give me the grace to change, never rejecting me because of my weakness. Let me continue to pursue my own path of change, knowing that I am responsible only to You and to myself. Remind me that the only way I can change anyone else is by my own example.*

4. Determine how to react to angering situations by changing your usual response and thus breaking the destructive pattern that anger has taken in the past. PRAY: *Father, now that I have decided to change with Your help, show me how to change! I am caught in a cycle: my responses to fear and the other things that feed my anger have always been pretty much the same . . . and they've gotten me nowhere I want to go! Help me to know—ahead of time while I am alone, quiet and rational—how I can better respond to*

upsetting situations. Allow me to teach myself simple, calm and clear responses that will break the cycles of the past. Give me the perseverance to regularly practice these prayerful responses so that I am more prepared when anger and fear strike. Stay with me as I put these lessons into practice. Let me remember that You are always with me, strong and quiet, lending me strength.

5. Maintain your new attitude and actions when those around you continue their old behavior. PRAY: *Lord of the past, present and future, keep me solidly on my road to peace and resolution. Those around me are resisting my changes. It even seems that they are trying to provoke me into changing back into the old ways. By changing my own responses, I have altered my relationship with those around me, and they are unhappy with this. Help me to stay calm and focused, Lord. Let me remember that I can change only myself, and that others may not always react the way I'd hoped.*

While Dr. Lerner rightly focuses on changing the self, for the man or woman of faith, empathy for others can be another key to dissipating anger. There's no better practical way to live a godly life than to try to understand the feelings and motives of others, including—and especially—those who are at the center of your fear and anger. This is not the same as "giving in" to inappropriate demands, or allowing yourself to be tempted away from the positive, prayerful actions you are taking to end the cycle of anger. Empathy is never a surrender to negativity; it is simply making the effort to understand the perspective and the life history of others so that you can act toward them with compassion. Understanding what is going on in the minds of others can also go a long way toward helping you to maintain your own program of prayerful action.

Prayer for Empathy

Even—especially—in the midst of trying to address your fear and anger, you can pray for the grace to develop empathy:

Compassionate Father, You know how fear and anger
tear at my spirit,
and claw at my heart and mind.
Help me, Lord, to remember that You created all of us,
including those who are causing me distress.
Whether I like it or not, whether I want to admit it or not,
these, too, are my brothers and sisters.
Keep that knowledge in my heart and mind.
Let it work against my fear and anger.
Quiet my distress long enough for me to see the sorrows, fears,
angers plaguing their lives.
Help me to see things from their perspectives.
Give me the gift of understanding.
Calm me long enough to hear and feel Your whispering voice,
urging me to be at peace with my fellow creatures.

Too often, those we find it most difficult to empathize with are those closest to us. It's always a tragedy when family relationships are rent by fear and anger. After all, the employer, neighbor, committee leader, coach, teacher, even pastor with whom we are angry is not someone who is supposed to love and accept us no matter what. The term *unconditional love* has caused a lot of trouble in relationships! It's virtually impossible for human nature to "grow" the delicate flower called unconditional love. Some of us may come close, but we are by nature needy, and it's very hard for us to love someone without requiring anything in return. To expect that someone—anyone, no matter how close to us—will love us regardless of how we act or how we treat that person borders on the ridiculous. And yet we've been taught that this is the kind of love we ought to expect to give and receive within our families.

Only God can truly love us unconditionally. You need to remember this when dealing with anger in your family. One of the first and best things you can do is to lower your expectations. One of the reasons that anger within a family is so debilitating is that we expect too much from one another. It is perfectly possible for members of the same family to be so different and to have so little in common, that simple courtesy and respect at the occasional family gathering is all that can be asked. When children are raised in difficult or unhealthy situations, it is unlikely that they will be happy as adults. Nor will the relationship between aging parents and adult children always be smooth or uncomplicated.

Many books have been written about the causes of fear and anger in families; resolving that fear and anger is another matter. Deep divisions in a family can make it seem as though even God cannot help. After all, many of us grow up thinking that family love is the closest thing to God's love that we can know on Earth.

When you're dealing with family conflict, remember Jesus' promise to the disciples:

> *"I will not leave you orphaned; I am coming to you . . . .*
> *On that day you will know that I am in my Father, and*
> *you in me, and I in you . . . . those who love me will be*
> *loved by my Father. . . ."*   —JOHN 14:18, 20–21

And when Jesus was informed that His family was looking for Him, He clarified His promise:

> *"Who are my mother and my brothers?" And looking at*
> *those who sat around him, he said, "Here are my*
> *mother and my brothers! Whoever does the will of God*
> *is my brother and sister and mother."*   —MARK 3:33–35

Jesus was not urging us to reject our families and our parents. However, He was trying to impress upon us the truth that *no* sibling, *no* parent, is the equal of the Son and the Father. As a man, Jesus was part of a family; He understood completely the potential for neediness, demands and even pettiness in the family structure. Yet in this passage Jesus is not denigrating the human family; rather He is reassuring us that when our human families fail us, and when we fail them (as they and we often do in one way or another), our heavenly Father will never fail. Indeed, Jesus is suggesting to us that if we have the same expectations of our families and parents that we have of God, we are bound to be disappointed. By confusing the very human love of family with the unfathomably boundless love of God, we create a situation where anger and resentment are likely to result.

When family love is tainted by anxiety and rage or when it fails altogether, it's easy to imagine that God has let us down too, or that He simply doesn't care about what we're going through. This is not true, and to the extent that such thoughts cause us to give up on prayer, they are plainly dangerous. When we are involved in a painful, angry family situation, we need prayer more than ever; and we need to understand that God loves us beyond any manner in which our families can love us. God loves us unconditionally, and it is to Him that we should turn when we feel let down, exhausted, even frightened by our families.

SURRENDER-AS-PRAYER

Nothing is more debilitating, more damaging to our sense of being loved and accepted, than longstanding family conflict. Eventually, we can lose all sense of clarity, of self-value. We can't understand why these angry, fearful, humiliating family situations continue; we don't know what we're doing wrong. Family fear and anger can rob us of all perspective, and we stubbornly refuse to surrender the pain and sorrow to God. Yet this very surrender can be the most profound kind of prayer in disturbing, unresolved situations. It is a way of saying, "Father, I just can't do this anymore. I don't even know *what* to do! I'm confused and frustrated. My sense of self-worth as Your child whom You have created for good is slipping away. Lord, I'm at my wit's end. I need to give up the control over this. I need to surrender the situation to You, Lord."

Surrender-as-prayer is not easy. Whether confronted with a distressing family conflict or in any other unresolved fear and anger, it's not easy to give up control, even to God. For some of us, surrender may be seen as a sign of weakness, inability or even laziness—I've struggled with surrender myself for these very reasons. I raised my eyebrows whenever anyone said "I just gave it up to God" when describing a problem or difficulty. I'd think, *Ah yes, the easy way out; let's dump all our problems on God.* Or I'd decide, *That's fine for you, but I know that God wants me to handle this myself.*

I still think that God provides us with the ability to address many of our problems, including anger and fear. It's just that sometimes, the best thing we can do—the way God is leading us—is to surrender. To consider the call to surrender a way of ducking responsibility, the way I sometimes did, was really just giving in to my pride. I kept telling myself that if I prayed hard enough for a solution (usually a solution I myself proposed to God!), for knowledge, for patience, for goodness, my prayer would be answered. It took me a long time to realize that when no specific answer came, when no solution materialized, that this very absence was in itself an answer.

In the situations where I've finally managed to admit that I am helpless, that I can't cope, that I can't find any path to resolution, I've learned to surrender to God. It hasn't been a simple matter for me: I have to ask God over and over again to give me the grace to let go of the situation before I can actually do it. I'm still working on surrender-as-prayer, but I've glimpsed the joy that comes with such complete trust, and it is worth the effort. Surrender to God is truly the ultimate faith resolution.

The decision to surrender doesn't automatically wipe out all fear and anger. Quite the contrary; surrender allows us to acknowledge and admit our fear and anger, and to realize that we cannot resolve it. For surrender to work, we must truly release our fear and anger. It's not enough just to say, "Lord, please take this from me." We must say with our heart and mind and spirit, "Lord, I give this up to You." Unless we're experienced in the prayer of surrender, it's unlikely we will feel immediately free of our burden. Surrender, like any other prayer, must be practiced. Our feelings will need to catch up with our will. We will need to seek clarity even through the remaining fog of fear and anger.

PRAYER FOR RELEASE FROM ANGER

In humility, comprehending your own weakness, pray that God will grant you the grace of surrender and take away your burden of fear and anger:

Almighty Father, let me accept my weakness, my failure,
my inability.
Allow me to turn my anger and fear over to You.
Lord, I can't carry it around anymore.
The weight is crushing me.
But it's so hard to let go, Lord!
It's not in my stubborn nature.
I think I should be able to handle this anger.
I tell myself I should be able to control this fear.
But Father, I know that without You, I can do nothing.
Help me to fully accept this truth.
Give me the grace to finally, completely, give my fear and
anger and hatred over to You.
Teach me that You are always waiting, ready to take these
crushing burdens from me.
Let me taste the sweetness of relief.
Let me walk with my shoulders straight, my head high,
knowing that my bonds have been broken in the glory
of Your strength.

APPRECIATIVE INQUIRY AS PRAYER

Addressing fear and anger in a prayerful way requires change. If what we've been doing worked, we wouldn't be stuck in these negative cycles, struggling even to pray. It may seem simpleminded to say that the best antidote to a negative cycle is positive thinking, but it's also quite often true. Appreciative Inquiry is a process for change that emphasizes the positive aspects of a situation by asking useful, "appreciative" questions, and then seeks to build in change by using answers. Developed by David Cooperrider and his associates at Case Western Reserve University as an alternative to the traditional way of making change by first focusing on what is wrong with a situation or institution, Appreciative Inquiry asks the question, "What is working well in this situation; what is right about this institution?" and then creates change based on the answers to these affirmative queries.

Though it might seem counterintuitive—how can we frame any positive questions, much less find positive answers, in the midst of crippling anxiety and anger?—Appreciative Inquiry can help you to work through situations of fear and anger and bring you back to sincere, effective prayer.

What would happen if you asked yourself new questions about your fear and anger, questions designed to seek out what is right about your situation, rather than what is wrong?

These questions in and of themselves would constitute the beginning of prayer; their answers would move you more deeply into prayer; and the eventual change in your attitude would help keep you focused on your prayer journey.

Start by simply thinking about the good things in your life and creating questions around these good things. For example, pray:

> *Father, help me to tune into the many good things in my life as I undertake this Appreciative Inquiry as Prayer. Keep my mind focused on the positive, and help me to resist falling into the old familiar negative thinking that has not worked in the past. Give me the courage to ask hopeful questions and create change.*

Then consider these questions (be sure to add your own as they occur to you):

- Why is my faith still so important to me?

- What makes me happy?

- How am I courageous?

- What makes me feel peace?

- Where am I most at peace?

- What prayers in the past have helped me?

- What positive words and images do I associate with God?

- Where do I feel closest to God?

- What have I heard or read that can help me in my situation?

- What positive things can I say about the person or people whom I fear and/or for whom I feel anger?

- Whom do I admire for the way he or she deals with fear, anger and conflict? What does he or she do that I admire most?

- What words of Jesus might be helpful for me now?

- What psalms apply to me in a useful way right now?

- How do I envision my best life in the future?

In answering these questions, give thanks for the answers and the positive change to which they can lead you if you are willing to follow. By investigating the questions in an affirmative way, you can formulate positive responses that will lead to active, prayerful ways of coping with and even resolving fear/anger situations.

For me, the answers to the question, "What prayers in the past have helped me?" would include:

1. Saying the Our Father slowly while I think about the meaning of every phrase.

2. Asking God to assist me to release my anger and fear.

3. Asking the Lord to forgive me for the negative ways I have expressed my fear and anger.

If your answers are similar to mine, you can build on them by taking prayerful actions like these:

1. Find a quiet place to say the Our Father. When you reach the phrase, "forgive us our trespasses as we forgive those who trespass against us," stop and think about what this means: *Yes, there are people I need to forgive, but most of them may feel that I need forgiveness from them.* Envision what it would be like if you managed to forgive each other. Using these new thoughts and perspectives, try to change the negative cycle.

2. Every morning when you wake up, ask God to help you to release your fear and anger to Him today—just this one day—trusting that He will take this burden from you if you don't hold on to it so tightly. Work to stay aware of the need to release your anger whenever you become aware of it during the day, asking for God's help as often as necessary. You might even try flexing your fingers in a "letting go" gesture when you begin to feel afraid and angry.

3. Every night before you go to bed, ask God to forgive you for the fear and anger you've shown that day. Make this presleep prayer knowing that God is ready, willing and able to forgive you—much more than you may be

willing to forgive yourself or others. Then, deliberately and calmly recall the day's moments of fear and anger, and ask God to forgive you for each of them and to remove the sting of pain you may have caused others. Fall asleep in the certainty that God has forgiven you, and that He's cheering you on for the days to come.

TRANSFORMATION

In the struggle with fear and anger (and for that matter, with anything else that can be an obstacle to our continuing conversation with God), it's hard to imagine that we will ever be able to banish these painful emotions from our lives. We do well to remember that our transformation is the work of God; when it happens to us, it will be His gift.

There is no greater example of this God-given transformation from fear and anger to peace and comprehension than Jonah. Called by God to preach to the sinful citizens of Nineveh, Jonah is seized by both fear of the responsibility and anger at the assignment—he doesn't think the Ninevites deserve saving—and so,

> *Jonah set out to flee to Tarshish from the presence of the Lord. He went down to Joppa and found a ship going to Tarshish; so he paid his fare and went on board, to go with them to Tarshish, away from the presence of the Lord.* —JONAH 1:3

But God does not give up on Jonah. To "persuade" Jonah, God causes a storm to rage around the ship in which Jonah is hiding. When the crew discovers that Jonah is fleeing from God, they take his despairing advice and throw him overboard, whereupon God sends a "large fish" to swallow him whole.

Jonah gets the hint. Once in the belly of the fish, Jonah suddenly remembers how to pray.

> *Then Jonah prayed to the Lord his God from the belly of the fish, saying, "I called to the Lord out of my distress, and he answered me . . . . As my life was ebbing away, I remembered the Lord; and my prayer came to you, into your holy temple."*   —JONAH 2:1–2, 7

The Lord, of course, hears the prayer that He's been waiting for from His stubborn prophet and allows the fish to spit Jonah upon the dry land. Again, God directs Jonah to Nineveh to preach repentance. This time Jonah goes and completes his mission so well that Nineveh converts humbly to the Lord.

You might think that Jonah had learned his lesson. But no. Even after he prays, and God delivers him, Jonah almost immediately collapses back into outbursts of anger. In what reads as a profound test of God's patience, Jonah is angry that God has had mercy on the Ninevites and allowed them to convert.

This was very displeasing to Jonah, and he became angry. He prayed to the Lord and said, "O Lord! Is not this what I said while I was still in my own country? That is why I fled . . . for I knew that you are a gracious God and merciful, slow to anger, and abounding in steadfast love, and ready to relent from punishing."

—JONAH 4:1–2

Here we see the destructive power of anger: Jonah sulks, angry with God for His mercy to the Ninevites. Yet just when we think God might lose all patience, God allows a sheltering bush to grow to shield Jonah from the burning heat. When God withers the plant, Jonah goes into a rage, but God uses Jonah's fury to teach him a transforming lesson.

But God said to Jonah, "Is it right for you to be angry about the bush?" And he said, "Yes, angry enough to die." Then the Lord said, "You are concerned about the bush, for which you did not labor and which you did not grow; it came into being in a night and perished in a night. And should I not be concerned about Nineveh, that great city, in which there are more than a hundred and twenty thousand people who do not know their right hand from their left, and also many animals?"

—JONAH 4:9–11

Jonah's story is a story of transformation. If we see ourselves in Jonah—our distress, anger, fear, pettiness, bigotry, loss of control, foolish second-guessing of God and just plain orneriness—we can also see how God never gives up on us. If God is willing to remake us despite ourselves, how much happier the journey if we choose to walk hand in hand with the Lord!

THANKSGIVING

As we've seen in so many cases, fear and anger can get in the way of clear thinking, but expressing appreciation to God can provide much-needed clarity. No matter how frightened or enraged we might be about other matters, we cannot deny that God deserves our thanks in so many ways. These prayers are designed to help you acknowledge the God Who is infinitely more powerful than your anger and fear.

Almighty God, thank You for showing me that anger can be overcome in the ultimate act of forgiveness You gave us in Your Son.

Jesus, Conqueror, thank You for showing us that You comprehend our human anger when You cleansed the temple of the money changers.

Father, thank You for the moments today when I managed to overcome my anger and show tolerance.

Dear Lord, thank You for showing me how much damage my anger can do and helping me to learn from those experiences.

Almighty God, thank You for the people in my life who encourage me to examine my emotions and practice peace.

PSALM-AS-PRAYER

When we are consumed by anger or fear, we need most to know that God is always with us. In its exceptionally beautiful imagery, this psalm describes how God sticks with us, regardless of how unworthy we feel or how far we think we've moved away from Him. And He simply doesn't let us be until we turn back to Him. What a comfort!

PSALM 139:1–12
THE INESCAPABLE GOD

O Lord, you have searched me and known me.
You know when I sit down and when I rise up;
you discern my thoughts from far away.
You search out my path and my lying down,
and are acquainted with all my ways.
Even before a word is on my tongue,
O Lord, you know it completely.
You hem me in, behind and before,
and lay your hand upon me.
Such knowledge is too wonderful for me;
it is so high that I cannot attain it.
Where can I go from your spirit?

Or where can I flee from your presence?
If I ascend to heaven, you are there;
if I make my bed in Sheol, you are there.
If I take the wings of the morning
and settle at the farthest limits of the sea,
even there your hand shall lead me,
and your right hand shall hold me fast.
If I say, "Surely the darkness shall cover me,
and the light around me become night,"
even the darkness is not dark to you;
the night is as bright as the day,
for darkness is as light to you.

SUGGESTED CLOSING PRAYER

Father, You know how I feel. You alone can see clearly the anger and fear that plague me. Teach me to seek refuge in You when I am troubled by these violent emotions. Keep me from hurting others and myself. Show me how to use the energy I waste on these feelings to achieve change in my life, my community and my world. Remind me always of the power of love. Let me learn the value of active prayer, and thus, end the cycle of useless hostility in my emotions and behavior.

BIBLE REFERENCE

Put away from you all bitterness and wrath and anger and wrangling and slander, together with all malice, and be kind to one another, tenderhearted, forgiving one another, as God in Christ has forgiven you. Therefore be imitators of God, as beloved children, and live in love, as Christ loved us and gave himself up for us, a fragrant offering and sacrifice to God.

—EPHESIANS 4:31—5:1–2

When Dangers Threaten

THESE DAYS, the world seems a dangerous place. We've grown accustomed to twenty-four-hour cable news reports of terrorist cells, bombings, threats, security procedures and evacuations because "a suspicious white powder was discovered in the mailroom." It's frightening how rapidly events like these have become a part of our daily lives.

Shortly after September 11, 2001, my husband Charlie and I boarded a plane for a long-scheduled cross-country trip. We had debated for weeks whether we should take the trip at all; we lived in Connecticut, and the reverberations of the attack had been felt in our state both in terms of personal loss and the heightened need for security. We'd spent some terrifying hours on September 11 waiting for a call from Charlie's stepdaughter, who worked in Manhattan. People in the small town where we lived gathered on the town green as if to make sure all the townspeople were accounted for. The church bells rang mournfully, and we all wondered how it could be such a clear, bright, beautiful day. There was little comfort we could give one another.

By the end of that week, Charlie and I were both shell-shocked, and we almost decided to cancel our long-anticipated trip to San Francisco. After all, the Golden Gate Bridge was suddenly considered a target, and the security throughout San Francisco was reported to be very tight. We weren't even sure we would find the same exciting, interesting city we'd grown to love. And, of course, flying out of New York would be no picnic, either. To add to our worries, ours was to be a direct flight, the kind authorities suspected that the terrorists had deliberately sought because nonstop, cross-country flights required so much combustible fuel.

But we'd already canceled a trip to the theater in New York City in late September, and the bleak, weary disappointment in the voice of the ticket agent when I called to cancel still echoed in my mind as we discussed the San Francisco trip. I'm not the bravest person in the world, but it seemed to us that to change our plans out of fear would be capitulating to the terrorists. And there was something else behind our decision to go: We didn't want fear and suspicion to rule—or ruin—our lives. We felt that a decision to stay home would be in some way a demonstration of a lack of faith.

Yet as we waited in the airport, two hours ahead of our flight, to go through the new security drill, I wasn't quite sure how to pray. Oh, I always prayed for safe travel when Charlie began his daily commute and whenever either of us went on a trip. I'm not the most eager flier under normal circumstances, but this was starkly different. The usual prayers simply did not flow from my mind and tongue. Somehow, they didn't seem to be enough. I felt that something more was required, but what? How could I pray in the face of such a massive assault on our country, our lives, our consciousness? How could I ask God for protection when so many were already dead and grieving? How could I express my confusion and frustration? As our flight began to board, I began to silently murmur an almost childlike, two-word phrase: *Please, Lord.*

We shuffled through the boarding tunnel. "Look at the size of this plane!" Charlie said softly. It was one of the huge double-decker planes that are usually reserved for a transcontinental flight and seldom used in a simple cross-country flight like ours. We'd taken many flights to California, but never in this kind of plane. The flight attendants— more numerous than we'd even seen before—urged us to sit wherever we would be comfortable, since the flight was far from full. "Bet this thing holds plenty of fuel," one older man commented nervously to his anxious wife. She ducked her head, not replying.

Please, Lord.

When we were belted in, the attendants did their best to calm our fears, addressing our concerns as tactfully as possible. "We know this is a difficult time and we very much appreciate your choosing our airline. As you can see, we will be traveling in comfort today: all the airlines are readjusting their schedules because of the drop in flights and we got the luck of the draw on this trip," said a pleasant, uniformed young man. After pointing out the unexpected luxuries of the aircraft which included a large video map of our route that kept Charlie mesmerized, individual movie screens, plenty of leg room and entire rows available for those who wanted to sleep (as if anyone could), the steward added, "Please be sure to let us know if you have any questions or concerns." A dark-skinned man in a turban who was traveling with his wife glanced uncomfortably around at his neighbors. Some did not return his gaze while others watched him suspiciously. His wife kept her eyes averted. His eyes held the same fear that I felt.

Please, Lord.

Please, Lord, what? I'm not sure I knew the answer, but as I kept repeating the prayer, I realized where I'd first heard it uttered. My old friend Maryann, the Irish lady I often visited in a local convalescent home, habitually murmured a prayer like this one. When I would assure her I'd be back next week, she'd breathe, "Please, God," as I brushed my lips against her dry cheek. When I told her that Charlie was on his way home from a trip, she'd say "Please, God," as if I were not there and she was appealing directly to the Father. When I wished her a happy birthday and reminded her that she was to be taken to spend the day with her best friend, she would close her eyes and say, "Please, God." At first I thought it was a charming plea, that she was asking God for these things she desired to transpire successfully: for me to return next week, for Charlie to come home safely, for her nonconvalescent home birthday celebration to go off without a hitch.

And it's true: she *was* appealing to God for these events. But I gradually understood that there was something more in Maryann's "Please, God." She was uttering a deeper prayer, in essence saying, "Let this thing happen, God, if it is *Your* will; if this thing that I want pleases *You*, then let it happen." I've come to understand that she was really saying, "Lord, please Yourself!" I'd never imagined that two words could mean so much, that a two-word prayer could be such an expression of total faith.

On our trip to San Francisco, when I said, "Please, Lord," I meant, "Please, Lord ... everything!" *Please, Lord, let there be no angry, desperate people on this plane. Please, Lord, let the plane contain no device that can damage it or force it to crash. Please, Lord, let the pilots be alert, courageous and experienced. Please, Lord, keep Charlie and me safe, and if we can't be safe, take us together. Please, Lord, don't let me become the kind of person who rejects my brothers and sisters out of my own fear. Please, Lord, bless that frightened man and his wife.*

The flight went off without a hitch, and, unsurprisingly, it was one of the smoothest, most luxurious flights we'd ever taken. By the time we were over the Midwest, most of the passengers had loosened up, and a few were even enjoying themselves. The rigidity in the shoulders of the turbaned man had relaxed, though the solemn, almost sorrowful, look on his face when we deplaned was the first real inkling I had of how deeply terrorism had set down roots in our world and how many victims it would claim.

Please, Lord.

GOD'S HANDS

As much as this reverent two-word prayer helped me through that trip, 9/11 was just the beginning of the era of heightened terrorism. While the initial horror and chaos gradually faded for many of us who were not hurt ourselves or did not lose loved ones, a new sense of confusion and sorrow settled into our hearts and lives. It seemed we lived under an anxious pall, never sure where the next crisis, the next tragedy would take place. Who would be the next victim? Would it be a bomb or a white powder or a chemical? Were the trains, buses and subways safe? Were our friends and relatives safe? The terror level changed colors faster than we could remember what each color meant. The trust that life was going to be okay practically evaporated into thin air.

Such a devastating event and its aftermath was bound to have an impact on faith. At first people flocked to special services to pray for the victims of the attack. All of us felt for them, and our hearts turned as one in prayer for them. Then, as the reverberations of the attack began to be felt, the prayers altered slightly. We found ourselves led in prayers that were as much for the country as for the victims. And this was fine. We love our country, and naturally we want God to bless and protect it. Gradually, as the United States engaged in what would become a protracted economic and military war against terrorism, those prayers began to be less about God helping the victims and protecting the nation, and more about God making the country victorious.

Soon, divisions began to make themselves evident among people of faith. Some prayed for peace at any cost; some prayed for justice—whatever that might mean for them; others prayed for victory; and still others prayed as the Israelites of old for God to destroy the enemy—whomever that might be. After the war in Iraq began, faith communities all over the country were split apart, sometimes deeply. Some were even at enmity with one another. Parishioners and congregants left or changed churches. Near my home in Connecticut, the presence of a submarine base only heightened the tension, and some Navy families made very public exits from churches where pastors were preaching against the war.

In this context I've reconsidered the difference between Maryann's "Please, God," and my "Please, Lord." I've come to understand that my prayer was, if not too selfish, then at least too self-absorbed. I was praying for safety for me and mine, with an occasional slight nod to others. I know this was natural, but I think that this sort of self-centered prayer can lead us to forget Who God is and to start treating Him

as One Who should do our bidding. All of a sudden we—
each of us—knows best; we know what God should do for
us, for the world, and we're convinced that if God does
what's best for us, it will be what's best for the world.

The truth is that if God answered the self-centered
prayers of everyone, very few of us would be happy with the
resulting chaos. For each of us to get our heart's desire from
God, we have to change our hearts. We have to undergo the
kind of transformation that God worked in Jonah. We have
to turn our hearts and minds to God, and pray that only His
will be done. We would have to pray as Maryann prayed,
"Please, God . . . O Lord, let what pleases You be done, for
whatever pleases You is what is perfect."

This doesn't mean we should stop praying for ourselves,
for each other, for safety, for peace, for justice. Those are all
worthy, and very natural, prayers. But we must leave the
specifics to God. We must put ourselves and our world—all
creations of God—into the hands of the Creator.

Praying for Leaders

"Please, Lord" and "Please, God" are legitimate prayer
responses to terrorism and the life we must live in this age of
terrorism. Still, these and other prayers require an active and
vigilant faith. Terrorism is not the only disturbing situation
we encounter in today's world. Hatred, poverty, violence and
despair are all too evident all over the world. We need only

look to the seemingly insolvable conflict in Israel and Palestine; the poverty, genocide and epidemic disease in Africa; the political instability in South and Central America; the bigotry and the widening gap between rich and poor that still exists in our country; and the nuclear build-up in Iran and North Korea.

In just the past decade, we've witnessed brutal genocide in a number of new and old nations; the wildfire spread of HIV; corruption and confrontation in the United Nations; devastating tsunamis, hurricanes and similar natural disasters; and violent insurgency in Iraq and Afghanistan. And at the time we most need unified government, world leaders and those in our own nation are deeply divided.

Praying for local, national and world leaders can be a comforting, useful practice during such trying times. Many churches include in their regular services prayers for the president, governor, congressmen and women, members of local government and church leaders. Such prayers need not be limited to church. Any individual or group can focus on prayers for leaders, especially leaders confronting difficult and complicated situations. We can make such prayers part of our regular routine, altering the daily petition to encompass specific events.

When you pray for leaders and governments, it may be helpful for you to remember a few guidelines. Asking God to give leaders the grace and discernment to recognize and do His will is more humble and potentially less divisive than praying for a specific outcome. Remember that we cannot know the ways of God or what He intends in any given crisis; we can only pray that our leaders open themselves to God's will and seek to accomplish it. Also, it may be useful to observe that Christians, Jews and Muslims all pray to the God of Abraham. Finally, we should not limit ourselves to praying only for those leaders who espouse our particular point of view. *All* leaders need prayers, and the humility inherent in praying for those we don't like or agree with is a sign of grace.

Here are models of the kinds of simple daily prayers you may use when you are troubled by the state of the world. Each can be tailored to specific events or problems.

Father, guide our president and Congress. Fill them with grace and discernment so that they may see Your way and pursue Your will in these troubling times. Teach them to work together for the good of all.

Provident God, I pray for all who lead the churches that they may be true and faithful ministers of your Word and Sacraments. Give them the courage to speak when You would have them speak, and to be silent when You would have them be silent. Help them to put aside their human desires and give themselves totally to Your will.

Lord, I know that on the Cross You suffered for all Your children. Forgive us and our leaders for those times during which we have forsaken Your way. Show us Your mercy as of old and lead the rulers in this world to the right path. Give me the courage to follow those who follow You.

Lord, I pray for our governor, city and county leaders, state lawmakers and judges. Touch them with Your love and wisdom. Give them the grace to act according to the dictates of Your compassion and justice. Protect them from all harm as they do their very difficult work.

God of all people, bless and protect the leaders of the world. Teach them to listen, first to You, and then to one another. Keep them from any path that damages Your creation; rather, teach them to nurture and protect Your people and the whole earth.

If you find it difficult to pray regularly for today's leaders, it may be helpful to pray by reading about the struggles and hopes of early Christian leaders. The Acts of the Apostles recounts how these men and women established Christianity in the face of strong opposition. Their determination and bravery can be of great comfort. Following the Acts, the letters of the apostles reveal the struggles, thoughts and unsurpassable faith of men like Paul, Peter, John and James. These potent and sometimes very personal letters can also teach us compassion for leaders who undertake the heavy burdens of governance.

In the early days of the church, the apostles were arrested and imprisoned many times for teaching the way of Jesus. At one point after being imprisoned, the apostles were brought

> . . . [to] stand before the council. The high priest questioned them, saying, "We gave you strict orders not to teach in this name, yet here you have filled Jerusalem with your teaching and you are determined to bring this man's blood on us." But Peter and the apostles answered, "We must obey God rather than any human authority. The God of our ancestors raised up Jesus . . . . [and] exalted him at his right hand as Leader and Savior so that he might give repentance to Israel and forgiveness of sins." . . . When they heard this, they were enraged and wanted to kill them.   —ACTS 5:27–31, 33

Later, we read,

> When they had called in the apostles, they had them flogged. Then they ordered them not to speak in the name of Jesus, and let them go. As they left the council, they rejoiced that they were considered worthy to suffer dishonor for the sake of the name. And every day in the temple and at home, they did not cease to teach and proclaim Jesus as the Messiah.   —ACTS 5:40–42

Threats of physical violence from the authorities were hardly the only challenges faced by early church leaders. Their spirits and beliefs were tested in the process of conversion.

As we experience the sometimes painful conversion of our own spirits and closely held beliefs in these challenging times, we can take comfort by prayerfully following the agonizing transformation of Saul/Paul.

> *Meanwhile Saul, still breathing threats and murder against the disciples of the Lord . . . . as he was going along and approaching Damascus, suddenly a light from heaven flashed around him. He fell to the ground and heard a voice saying to him, "Saul, Saul, why do you persecute me?" He asked, "Who are you, Lord?" The reply came, "I am Jesus, whom you are persecuting. But get up and enter the city, and you will be told what you are to do." The men who were traveling with him stood speechless because they heard the voice but saw no one. Saul got up from the ground, and though his eyes were open, he could see nothing; so they led him by the hand and brought him into Damascus. For three days he was without sight, and neither ate nor drank.*   —ACTS 9:1, 3–9

Make no mistake about it, the apostles and disciples of the early Church lived in a time of terrorism. They were hunted, intimidated, attacked, brought to trial, condemned and even martyred. At the same time, their world was shaken by instability. The Romans felt themselves to be engaged in their own war of terror against the rebel Zealots, who were more than willing to die for a free Jerusalem. Early

Christians were accustomed to seeing rebels against Rome hanging, crucified, from trees along major roads. To add to the distress and chaos, there were false messiahs and prophets everywhere. Both the Jewish and Roman governments were rife with corruption and division. Religious leaders were at odds with one another about vital issues like how to deal with the Roman conquerors and how to address the challenge of the early Church.

Sound familiar? The challenges faced by early Church members and the valiant and prayerful attitude with which they responded can be of great consolation to us, especially as we seek to pray:

Jesus, You filled Your followers with determination and love.
Yet even they experienced fear and uncertainty
in times of terror.
They were hunted and persecuted,
beaten, accused, tried and even martyred.
But You transformed them, Jesus,
sending Your Spirit to them to comfort and guide them,
to protect and nurture them.
Through You, they were transformed.
They spoke in tongues,
healed the sick, raised the dead, forgave sinners.
They confounded their enemies, not with war,
but with the words You gave them.
Jesus, Lord, I am floundering!

In these dangerous days, I'm not sure what to do,
or even how to pray.
Let me take my inspiration from Your followers, Jesus.
Send Your Spirit upon me, O Lord!
Comfort me, protect me, teach me Your will.
Take from my heart and tongue any words of anger,
condemnation, judgment.
Replace them with Your way, Your Spirit, Your words.

UNDER GOD:
PRAYING FOR THE PEACE OF UNITY

It is important during times of war and violence to pray for peace as well as the necessary companion of peace, unity. As believers we must not forget for one moment that Jesus' message was one of love. Again and again and again, He stresses that His purpose is to inculcate love among His followers in imitation of the perfect love between Him and His Father. Though some of His disciples came to mistakenly believe that Jesus intended to overthrow the Roman occupiers of Jerusalem, He did everything in His power to show them that His kingdom had nothing to do with their concept of war or violence.

A lawyer asked him a question to test him. "Teacher, which commandment in the law is the greatest?" He said to him, "'You shall love the Lord your God with all your heart, and with all your soul, and with all your mind.' This is the greatest and first commandment. And the second is like it: 'You shall love your neighbor as yourself.' On these two commandments hang all the law and the prophets." —MATTHEW 22:35–40

For God so loved the world that he gave his only Son, so that everyone who believes in him may not perish but may have eternal life. Indeed, God did not send the Son into the world to condemn the world, but in order that the world might be saved through him.

—JOHN 3:16–17

Little children . . . . I give you a new commandment, that you love one another. Just as I have loved you, you also should love one another. By this everyone will know that you are my disciples, if you have love for one another. —JOHN 13:33–35

Willful killing and destruction of life can have no rightful place in the hearts of those who follow Jesus. Yet we all get caught up in feeling patriotic, righteous about "our side." But war, as we see in the Gospels, is not what Jesus wanted; in fact, it is quite the opposite. He expressly rejected violence when He was threatened in the garden of Gethsemane:

Then they came and laid hands on Jesus and arrested him. Suddenly, one of those with Jesus put his hand on his sword, drew it, and struck the slave of the high priest, cutting off his ear. Then Jesus said to him, "Put

your sword back into its place; for all who take the
sword will perish by the sword. Do you think that I
cannot appeal to my Father, and he will at once send
me more than twelve legions of angels? But how then
would the scriptures be fulfilled, which say it must
happen in this way?" —MATTHEW 26:50–54

All too often in history, Christians have failed to heed Jesus' admonition against violence. How can the ruinous Crusades or the vicious pogroms against Jews in Europe and Russia stand up to Jesus' instruction?

"But I say to you, Love your enemies and pray for those
who persecute you, so that you may be children of your
Father in heaven; for he makes his sun rise on the evil
and on the good, and sends rain on the righteous and
on the unrighteous. For if you love those who love you,
what reward do you have? . . ." —MATTHEW 5:44–46

It takes courage to pray for peace and unity when we feel ourselves under the cloud of terrorism. Not only must we rise above our own fear and anger, we often must rise above our deeply ingrained prejudices and attitudes toward others, especially strangers. We do well to begin by asking God for the will to pray for peace and unity:

Father, help me to remember that You are the Father of all,
the Creator of all.

You promised Abraham that he and Sarah would found
a great nation;
You exceeded even Your promise,
for from Abraham grew up three great nations!
Christians, Jews and Muslims from all over the world claim
You as Father,
and Abraham as ancestor.
People in every corner of the earth,
people of every race and color,
people of every language and dialect,
people from every climate and every continent,
people who herd goats and people who herd nations,
people who may agree on little else—
all these people pray, like I do, to You, Father.
Help me to strive to overcome both ancient
and new differences, hatred, bigotries, fears,
so that I may pray sincerely for peace.

DOING WHAT CAN BE DONE

Active faith in an age of terrorism can be an important and
helpful way to stay engaged in life and in prayer. We may not
be able to solve all the global problems that cause terrorism,
or even protect ourselves and our loved ones from terrorist
acts, but we can make the decision to act positively, to "do
what can be done" to stand up to terrorism, to live faithfully

despite it. Active prayer can be any action taken with the words of Jesus and the love of God fixed firmly in our minds and hearts. Doing what can be done in the face of terrorism will encompass a wide range of loving, prayerful, and deeply personal actions that we take in a faithful effort to live the teachings of Jesus.

Positive thinking is a great way to start "doing what can be done." We are so inundated with negative news that it can take a major effort to turn around our thinking. I try to combat feelings of hopelessness about terrorism and the state of the world by keeping a mental scrapbook of "good news." This is a form of self-defense for me. With the constant barrage of negative reporting by the print and broadcast news media, I've found it both helpful and hopeful to keep track of the occasional good stories. I cherish them because they suggest there is some hope for us, hope for peace, hope for unity, hope that human beings are at least capable of acting like God's children and Jesus' siblings. Every item on my list can be seen, in and of itself, as a kind of prayer, an act of faith and courage.

My active prayer scrapbook started with the report a few years ago of how a building collapsed during a wedding in Israel, and, moved by their common humanity, both Palestinians and Israelis rushed into the rubble to try to rescue victims and help those who were trapped and confused. I comfort myself with the image of all those people, not caring and maybe even not knowing at least for that moment that they were enemies, running together into danger to help whomever they found. For that brief time, these ancient enemies acted like the brothers and sisters they might be.

Other media images that strike hope and courage in my heart include the Muslim doctor in Afghanistan who, when he discovered that some wounded and captured American soldiers were being held at a camouflaged hospital, took the great risk of informing the American military so that the prisoners of war could be freed; the very public handshake between the relatively new and young Syrian president, trying to separate himself from his father's brutal policies, and a highly placed Israeli government official; the surviving victims of 9/11 who publicly called for peace and not retribution despite their anguish; the commitment by Israel to pull out of disputed regions and to move as best they could toward a peaceful solution; the shared life in Sierra Leone between Muslims and Christians that allows for peace and a greater understanding between people of different faiths; reports that nations like Croatia on the Adriatic Sea and Libya on the Mediterranean, though recently plagued by brutal leadership and terror, are now working to put aside their recent history in order to build an economic base in tourism and trade.

Perhaps one of the most recent and poignant entries in my prayer scrapbook of hopeful news is the response of

Marie Fatayi-Williams to the murder of her twenty-six-year-old son Anthony, and more than fifty other people in the four London subway bombings on July 7, 2005. Mrs. Williams, a Catholic from Nigeria who lived and worked in London as did Anthony's father, a Muslim doctor, mourned for her only son in front of the whole world as she waited for the official word of his death. And the whole world doubtless would have understood if Mrs. Fatayi-Williams had called for revenge.

But Marie Fatayi-Williams, in the most terrible moment of her life, first acknowledged that she'd been "destroyed" by her son's murder. But then she said, "It's time to stop and think. We cannot live in fear because we are surrounded by hatred. Anthony is a Nigerian, born in London, worked in London, he is a world citizen. Here today we have Christians, Muslims, Jews, Sikhs, Hindus, all of us united in love for Anthony. Hatred begets only hatred. It is time to stop this vicious cycle of killing. We must all stand together, for our common humanity."

There are a number of prayer actions we can take in the spirit of "doing what can be done" to stand against terrorism and for peace and unity. Here are some suggestions:

- Send a "care package" to American troops stationed in Iraq or other "hot spots" throughout the world. These can include approved foods and practical items as well as cards, games, books and other things that will remind the servicemen and women in other countries of our thoughts and prayers.

↝ Try to learn something about a faith other than yours. Attend services at a place of worship other than yours. Take a study course. Spend time talking to someone from a different faith. Focus on those beliefs, traditions and moral values that you hold in common.

↝ Put yourself in the place of those living under the burden of daily terror. What if you were living in a society where you had to prove your faith by dying for it, or by killing others? What if your child couldn't attend school because terrorists had burned the local schools to the ground? Put yourself in the place of these people, and try to put aside for these few moments all that we, as Americans, take for granted.

↝ Pray for people living in specific situations where terror is a daily reality.

↝ Pray for the people of Afghanistan and Iraq who are still caught in the crossfire of terror and warfare as those countries attempt to establish new governments.

↝ Pray for the people of Israel and Palestine as they try to achieve a resolution amidst different terrorist factions seeking to disrupt the peace process.

↝ Pray for the families of American soldiers and the families of all soldiers fighting anywhere in the war on terrorism.

↝ Pray for all victims of terrorism and their families.

- Pray for all young people living in terror who are vulnerable to being convinced that their only path to power is to become terrorists themselves.

- Pray for all people who are vulnerable to believing that God approves of killing.

- Pray for the governments in nations like Iran, Iraq, Israel, Palestine, Afghanistan and other countries where leaders are often targets of assassination attempts.

- Pray for the people and leaders in nations such as Sierra Leone and Liberia that are trying to recover from civil wars that often devolved into reigns of terror.

- Donate money, goods or time to organizations that monitor progress or work to help the victims of terror like Americares, Amnesty International, Doctors Without Borders, CARE and UNICEF.

OTHER ACTIVE PRAYERS

Here are some other active prayers that I've benefited from myself or that others have graciously shared with me. Feel free to use any of these in your own journey as well as to create your own active prayer plans.

- When you feel especially beset by anxiety or hopelessness because of the distressing state of the world, take a walk with God. Try to find a pleasant place to walk, perhaps a beach, a park, a trail, a quiet road. Before you begin, invite

God to join you. Describe your state of mind to Him as you would to a beloved friend. As you walk, be conscious of God by your side. When your mind wanders, bring yourself back by softly repeating, "Lord, fill me with Your peace." If you need to, repeat this phrase constantly like a calming, prayerful refrain. Breathe deeply and walk with the confidence of God's presence.

- Read the Acts of the Apostles and the letters of Peter, Paul, James and John to get a sense of the kind of terror the early Christians experienced. Take comfort from their faith, commitment and determination to be a people of love, peace and unity.

- Consider starting a support or discussion group for people concerned about terrorism and the state of the world. The group can consist of two or three, or of twenty or thirty, and it can be organized in any number of ways and around a variety of themes. It can be simply a discussion group where people share their concerns. It can be a topical group where each gathering focuses on a specific issue or situation. It can be a reading group where the meetings target an article or book on an issue important to the group. The group can meet in the homes of individual members, a local church or library or at a cafe, restaurant or coffee shop. However the group is organized, each meeting should begin and end with a prayer, and discussions should be constrained by courtesy: Remember, the point is to support each other regardless of differing perspectives.

THANKSGIVING

A preoccupation with terrorism and negative world events can make it difficult for us to see all the wondrous aspects of life. These prayers concentrate on those good things and can be bolstered by your "Good News Scrapbook." These prayers may be altered to meet individual needs and to correspond with current "good news."

My Protector, thank You that today the people I love are safe.

Lord, thank You for the good news in the world that renews my faith in humanity.

Father, thank You for the outpouring of financial, physical and spiritual support that invariably occurs after a tragedy in our community or our world.

Dear Jesus, thank You for warning us that the world would be subject to war, natural disasters and unrest so that when these things occur, we are comforted by Your presence.

Glorious God, thank You for all those in the world who do the hard work of advancing peace, feeding the poor, healing the sick, easing anguish and preventing disasters.

Generous Father, thank You for providing me many opportunities to give my money and my time to organizations and individuals who are working for the good of all.

Loving Lord, thank You for the funny pages that provide us with relief from the news in the daily paper.

Jesus, beloved Brother, thank You for bringing me into the path of little children who renew my hope with their sense of play and their innocence.

PSALM-AS-PRAYER

Though many of the phrases in this psalm are familiar, it is particularly suited to those who feel trapped by global terrorism, destitution, discontent and war. In confronting such a deeply troubled world, it's easy to feel completely overwhelmed. Yet this psalm tells us that what appears impossible to us is well within God's power. God alone can save the world. God alone can save each and every one of us.

PSALM 71:1–16
PRAYER FOR LIFELONG PROTECTION AND HELP

In you, O Lord, I take refuge;
let me never be put to shame.
In your righteousness deliver me and rescue me;

Incline your ear to me and save me.
Be to me a rock of refuge,
a strong fortress, to save me,
for you are my rock and my fortress.
Rescue me, O my God, from the hand of the wicked,
from the grasp of the unjust and cruel.
For you, O Lord, are my hope,
my trust, O Lord, from my youth.
Upon you I have leaned from my birth;
it was you who took me from my mother's womb.
My praise is continually of you.
I have been like a portent to many,
but you are my strong refuge.
My mouth is filled with your praise,
and with your glory all day long.
Do not cast me off in the time of old age;
do not forsake me when my strength is spent.
For my enemies speak concerning me;
and those who watch for my life consult together.
They say, "Pursue and seize that person
whom God has forsaken,
for there is no one to deliver."
O God, do not be far from me;
O my God, make haste to help me!
Let my accusers be put to shame and consumed;
let those who seek to hurt me be covered
with scorn and disgrace.

But I will hope continually,
and will praise you yet more and more.
My mouth will tell of your righteous acts,
of your deeds of salvation all day long,
though their number is past my knowledge.
I will come praising the mighty deeds of the Lord God,
I will praise your righteousness, yours alone.

SUGGESTED CLOSING PRAYER

Lord, I am so discouraged by the state of our world. There is fear and danger everywhere. I don't know how to protect myself, my family, my friends. I don't know whom to trust, who to believe. I'm not even sure how to live in such a world. Let me see Your presence in the midst of all this, Lord! Teach me to remember how Your people throughout the ages have faced similar disturbing times, and grown closer to You. Give me the courage to persevere and to express that perseverance and love in my daily life. Let my life be a prayer, so that all may see Your work in me.

BIBLE REFERENCE

But the one who endures to the end will be saved.

—MATTHEW 10:22

When You Feel That You've Failed

WHEN YOU FEEL that you've failed at something important in life—your job, your marriage, parenting, beating an addiction, attaining financial independence—you may begin to believe that you've failed in God's eyes too. You may even assume that your failure is some sort of punishment for your sins and unworthiness, or that God doesn't want you to succeed, and you may then draw away from God because of feelings of shame or abandonment. You may also draw away from the people who love and support you—family, friends and church community—increasing your sense of isolation and loneliness. For more than three years, I've been facilitating a support group for believers of faith who are anxious or depressed. The group began with a talk I gave at the Waterford Public Library in Connecticut. In the audience that evening was an attractive, deeply tanned woman of about forty. She listened intently, watching me closely as I spoke. She told me after the talk that she was sure that God had sent her to the event. When she learned I'd be forming a support group, she was one of the first to sign up.

At our early meetings, she was very forthcoming. She felt that everything in her life had gone wrong: her child was very ill; her job was unpleasant and no one there seemed to understand what she was going through, so it was nearly impossible to get the time off she needed. Her husband was apparently of no help. She herself was sick much of the time, probably with stress- and anxiety-related illnesses. She felt she had nowhere to go, no one to turn to. She felt like a failure. And most of all, she felt that God had deserted her, that He was not helping her or even paying attention to her situation.

"Why do you think all this has happened to me?" she asked me after one of our meetings. "I pray and I pray and I pray. Isn't God listening? What do I have to do to get Him to listen to me? Why isn't He helping me?"

I racked my brain for something to say, something that might comfort her. She waited, keeping her eyes steadily on me. Finally I said, "Well, He is answering you. He sent you here to this group, didn't He? He sent you to be with people who are experiencing the same fears and hurts you are. He put you in a place where you could feel safe, at least for a couple of hours, talking about yourself and just being yourself."

She looked at me and then, slowly and sadly, she smiled. She nodded, as if I'd said just what she'd expected me to say, and it wasn't enough. My heart sank. We didn't see her again after that meeting.

Much later I asked my very wise friend Margaret, a strong advocate of Appreciative Inquiry, about this incident. I guess I was feeling a bit like a failure myself! "What should I have done or said?" I asked Margaret. "I felt so useless, as if nothing I could say would get through to her. And she was expecting so much."

Margaret suggested that if the woman ever returned, I should ask what was good or positive in her life. "Ask her what she likes about herself, about her life, about her work, about her family," Margaret advised. "Try to help her name at least one positive thing and then build off of that."

The more I thought about it, the more I realized that even Margaret's counsel might not have worked. The woman was not able to see anything that was positive in her life, and I'm not sure I could have shown it to her. Her responses to the few questions I did manage to ask were always negative. She seemed to return again and again to the idea that the "failures" in her life were somehow connected to God abandoning her.

HUMAN NATURE

It's part of our human nature to look for reasons for the negative things, the failures, in life. It's easier to handle failure when you can blame someone else. "If my co-worker wasn't always stealing my ideas and running to the boss with them, I'd have gotten that promotion. If my spouse would help out around the house, it wouldn't look like such a disaster area. If my friends were more flexible, I wouldn't have such a hard time maintaining relationships. If my kids would do what I tell them to do, they wouldn't be in trouble all the time. If my pastor were more understanding, I could go to him for counseling. If the doctor would only prescribe the right medicine, I'd feel so much better."

If. If. If. It's natural to look for reasons for what we perceive as the failures in our lives. And it's a short hop from blaming others to blaming God. It's easy to play the *If, If, If* game with God. "If God would only open the boss's eyes, I'd get that promotion. If God would only bless our marriage, things would be so much better. If God would only make the kids listen, I wouldn't feel so ineffective as a parent. If God would only improve my health, I wouldn't have to feel guilty about our poor diet and lack of exercise."

While it may be easy to think that God has abandoned you to failure, it is never true. Even when you can't understand why you're struggling with difficulties, God's will is for your ultimate good. And whether you blame yourself, others or God for the failures in your life, turning away from the Lord is never the right answer. In fact, by turning away from God, you are turning away from the source of hope, clarity and salvation.

If you feel that failure is a result of God's inattention or lack of care, you might want to consider some of the people in the Bible who experienced failure. Far from abandoning them, God made these magnificent failures into some of the most magnificent successes in the Scriptures.

Abraham sent his son and her mother into the desert to die. Sarah laughed scornfully at the angels who predicted her coming pregnancy. Jacob lied to his father, Isaac. Aaron made the Israelites a golden calf to worship. Miriam tried to lead the people away from Moses and God. David arranged to have the husband of Bathsheba killed in battle so that he might marry her. Solomon, despite God's gift of wisdom, allowed idolatry in Israel. Thomas doubted Jesus' power. Peter denied Jesus three times.

Perhaps the greatest example of a magnificent failure transformed by God into a magnificent success is Saul the Pharisee, whom we know as the apostle Paul. In the midst of hunting down the followers of Jesus, he is given a terrifying vision of Jesus and then is struck blind. Saul does not blame the Lord for his blindness, his fear. He does not say, "But Lord, I've been praying all my life, doing Your work all my life, how could You do this to me?" Rather, Saul says only, "Who are you, Lord?" The reply came, "I am Jesus, whom you are persecuting. But get up and enter the city, and you will be told what you are to do" (Acts 9:5–6). The Acts of the Apostles describes his reaction:

The men who were traveling with him stood speechless because they heard the voice but saw no one. Saul got up from the ground, and though his eyes were open, he

could see nothing; so they led him by the hand and
brought him into Damascus. For three days he was
without sight, and neither ate nor drank.   —ACTS 9:7–9

And then Saul waited for the Lord. In silence. In the dark. Hungry. Thirsty. Fasting. Until finally at the command of God,

Ananias went and entered the house. He laid his hands
on Saul and said, "Brother Saul, the Lord Jesus, who
appeared to you on your way here, has sent me so that
you may regain your sight and be filled with the Holy
Spirit." And immediately something like scales fell from
his eyes, and his sight was restored. Then he got up and
was baptized, and after taking some food, he regained
his strength.   —ACTS 9:17–19

From that moment on, God shaped Saul into one of the most powerful evangelists in the history of Christianity.

Immediately he began to proclaim Jesus in the syna-
gogues, saying, "He is the Son of God." All who heard
him were amazed and said, "Is not this the man who
made havoc in Jerusalem among those who invoked
this name? And has he not come here for the purpose of
bringing them bound before the chief priests?" Saul
became increasingly more powerful and confounded
the Jews who lived in Damascus by proving that Jesus
was the Messiah.   —ACTS 9:20–22

Paul never denied his failure, often telling the story how he had wrongly persecuted the early Christians. Later, when on trial, he tells King Agrippa and Queen Bernice,

"Indeed, I myself was convinced that I ought to do many things against the name of Jesus of Nazareth. And that is what I did in Jerusalem; with authority received from the chief priests, I not only locked up many of the saints in prison, but I also cast my vote against them when they were being condemned to death. By punishing them often in all the synagogues I tried to force them to blaspheme; and since I was so furiously enraged at them, I pursued them even to foreign cities . . . . I was not disobedient to the heavenly vision, but declared first to those in Damascus, then in Jerusalem and throughout the countryside of Judea, and also to the Gentiles, that they should repent and turn to God and do deeds consistent with repentance."

—ACTS 26:9–11, 19–20

No matter how utterly you think you've failed, your failures probably don't approach those of Saul/Paul, or for that matter, Old Testament kings like David. You can do no better than to follow their model of humble prayer and patience while waiting on the Lord. Keeping their examples in mind, you can pray:

Father, thank You for the Scriptures that reveal both the failures and successes of Your most faithful men and women. When I allow my failure to draw me away from You,

when I allow my failure to compel me to play the "blame game,"
when I allow my failure to make me a victim of myself,
remind me that I can pray by reading the Scriptures.
And as I pray and stay close to You by reading about
Your chosen ones,
help me to apply their experiences to my own.
As I struggle with my own weaknesses and failures,
teach me to demonstrate the humility of Jacob,
to sorrowfully admit my guilt as Aaron did,
to forcefully separate myself from my sins
in the manner of Miriam,
to pray for forgiveness as David did,
to proclaim repeatedly my love for You in imitation of Peter,
to acknowledge my worst failures and wait for Your
forgiveness and guidance as Paul did.
Let Your Word teach me that my failings need not
separate me from You.

SELF-BLAME VS. SELF-AWARENESS

Sometimes our most dangerous tendency when facing failure can be self-blame. When I learned, after six years of clean biopsies, that the cancer I thought was long gone had resurfaced, I was devastated. Although the new cancers, like the first, were blessedly caught and successfully removed in the very earliest stage, I found it all too easy to blame myself. *How have I failed?* I wondered. Modern medicine, the media, health-care gurus and even some religious leaders all seemed to be telling us that anyone who lived right, ate right, slept right, medicated right, meditated right and certainly prayed right could achieve good health. Knowledge about every aspect of healthy living was easily available; all I needed to do was take advantage of the many tests and diagnostic procedures to catch any problems early. It seemed that if I simply acted responsibly and had the right attitude, any illness could be avoided or eradicated.

So what had I done wrong? My diet was pretty good. I walked seven or eight miles a day; wasn't that enough? I wore enough sunscreen to make little children cross the street in fear when they saw me coming. I endured regular checkups, countless preventive biopsies, blood tests. I took my daily multivitamin. Maybe it was stress: I'd not exactly succeeded in eliminating that little problem.

Or was it that I hadn't prayed enough? Was God upset with me? Wasn't I paying enough attention? Was I too proud? Had I been unkind? Not doing enough good works? Too selfish? Had I taken too much for granted? Was this some kind of terrifying wake-up call?

I didn't truly believe that God was using cancer in order to punish me or alert me to my glaring failures. But I know that for me at least, faith is part thinking and part feeling, and the feeling part often lags far behind the thinking part. So although I firmly believed that God loved me and was not out to get me or cause me pain and sorrow, my feelings were another matter. Well aware of my many shortcomings, I couldn't keep myself from feeling, at least a little, that I'd done something wrong.

Worried that such negative thinking could draw me away from prayer, I took the red pen I reserved for prayer journaling and listed a series of prayer lessons that I still refer to when I feel like a failure. I began the exercise with one of the most comforting passages in Scripture, one that consistently reminds me of how deeply God loves us:

> *"For I know the plans I have for you," declares the Lord,*
> *"plans to prosper you and not to harm you; plans to*
> *give you hope and a future."*   —JEREMIAH 29:11 (NIV)

Then came my prayer lessons:

> *Praise the Lord!*
> *Remember always: God is healing me!*
> *I must choose trust and faith in God over fear.*
> *Obsessive, fearful prayer is not an expression of faith.*
> *Be calm.*
> *I must not allow my fear to let me be mean or judgmental.*
> *Not everyone knows what I am going through,*
> *nor should I expect them to. I will try to be kind.*
> *I will do what I love to do, avoid those things*
> *that cause me pain and anxiety and stop trying*
> *to defend or justify my choices.*
> *Faith feels better than fear!*
> *Trust feels better than fear!*
> *Simple, silent, hopeful prayer is faith.*

I must try to let go of what is negative and blaming.
These emotions, these feelings, are not helpful
and can only set me back.
I will keep my perspective about what really matters.
I will be honest with myself.
I will not whine!
Please Lord, be with me, stay with me.
Thank You, Lord.
God is healing me!
Praise the Lord!

While self-blame can be an obstacle to prayer and faith, refusing to acknowledge our weaknesses and negative behavior can be just as debilitating. In the same way that failure is seldom completely our fault, we are seldom completely without responsibility for the problems in our lives. By denying your own accountability, you can become trapped in negative patterns that can lead to bitterness and blame.

We cannot be healed, nor can we succeed, until we recognize where we are ill, where we have failed. God does not need us to name our faults for His sake; He is well aware of them because He is wounded for us and hurts with us. But He needs us to admit them to ourselves because only through self-examination and honesty can we prepare ourselves to turn to Him. We have seen how Saul/Paul at first failed the Lord, and then, acknowledging his failure and humbling himself before the Lord, was forged into a marvelous success.

The other Saul, ancient Israel's first king, provides the opposite model: God raised him up to the heights of success, but when Saul refused to admit his own failings, he plummeted miserably from those heights. No matter how many opportunities he was given to acknowledge his mistakes and seek help in changing his course, Saul refused. He allowed himself to be imprisoned in his own negative cycle, drawn farther and farther from the Lord.

It was Saul's failure of faith, offering a forbidden sacrifice rather than waiting for the prophet Samuel's help, that began his downfall. Rather than beg the Lord for forgiveness, Saul had all sorts of excuses:

> *Samuel said, "What have you done?" Saul replied, "When I saw that the people were slipping away from me, and that you did not come within the days appointed, and that the Philistines were mustering at Michmash, I said, 'Now the Philistines will come down upon me at Gilgal, and I have not entreated the favor of the Lord'; so I forced myself, and offered the burnt offering."*
>
> —1 SAMUEL 13:11–12

When Samuel responded that Saul had lost God's favor through this insult, and that the Lord would favor another over Saul, Saul began to indulge himself with envious conjecture.

The downward spiral continued as Saul disobeyed the Lord in other ways, still unable to take responsibility for the path he had set himself on. When Samuel, growing frustrated, confronted Saul after Saul had disobeyed God's command by confiscating the cattle and sheep of a conquered nation, Saul again made excuses.

> *Saul said to Samuel, "I have obeyed the voice of the Lord, I have gone on the mission on which the Lord sent me. . . . But from the spoil the people took sheep and cattle, the best of the things devoted to destruction, to sacrifice to the Lord your God in Gilgal."*
>
> —1 SAMUEL 15:20–21

Saul had begun referring to the Father as "the Lord *your* God," not "the Lord *my* God." He had separated himself from the Lord.

By the time Saul finally admitted his culpability, he was beyond hoping that the Lord would save him. Instead, he repents for the sake of appearances, telling Samuel,

> *"I have sinned; yet honor me now before the elders of my people and before Israel, and return with me, so that I may worship the Lord your God."*
>
> —1 SAMUEL 15:30

That's the problem with refusing to admit failure: we grow so accustomed to blaming others or making excuses, that we can lose sight of who we are and what we are doing. The painful contradictions multiply and the self-imposed confusion increases. We cannot be separate from God and still one with ourselves.

Things got even worse for Saul when David entered the scene. Loving and needing David as a substitute son, a healer and a warrior, Saul also knew that David was the one upon whom God's favor rested. And so Saul's resentment ate him alive.

It's human nature to avoid blame and shun accountability. I've been reminded of this recently in my own life. Not long ago, I was in a bad mood. I made excuses for myself—stress over a new project, fear of a recurrence of cancer, miserable weather, stymied plans. But the simple truth was that I wasn't feeling great about anything, including myself. And I took it out on my husband.

Now Charlie is one of the kindest, easiest-going guys on the face of the earth. So when the feeling of failure overtakes me, it's all too easy for me to "let it all out" because I know how understanding he is. But during this recent "down" period, I found myself snapping at him, and that's something we just don't do much. We try to be careful of one another's feelings, and, largely because of Charlie's general affability, we've had very little conflict. We've made it a practice to let the little things go by.

But that didn't stop me this time. I felt sorry enough for myself to suspend the unspoken rules in our house. Charlie, well-adjusted as always, pretty much ignored my impatience and the occasional snide comment. But one night, after making some unkind remark, I happened to look in his direction. The look on his face was a combination of pensiveness and hurt. I stopped in my tracks, breathed in sharply, and then, without another word, went over and hugged him.

I knew that God had gently tapped me on the shoulder so that I would turn around and look at my husband's face. It never really crossed my mind that my miserable attitude could hurt Charlie, and when I saw that it had, I was devastated.

That night, sleepless, I thought about everything that had happened. I realized that my behavior, instead of helping me to address my negative feelings, was just making them worse. My feeling of failure wasn't fading: it was intensifying.

Was I a failure in my marriage because of this brief period of negativism and mean behavior? No. But if I hadn't heeded God's call, if I hadn't looked carefully into the face of the one I loved so deeply, or worse, if after seeing the truth, I'd ignored it or made excuses for myself, my temporary lapse could have escalated into a full-blown failure.

It is so important to honestly examine your feelings and behaviors. If you are experiencing failure, or just the sense of impending failure, it is vital to stop and look at what's happening. God is providing you with the opportunity to evaluate your behavior, to see the impact it has on others, and, if necessary, to search for a new way. Self-blame is destructive, but self-denial can prevent us from rejecting the disastrous patterns that can ruin our lives and lead us farther from God.

This short prayer, asking for the courage to face failings honestly, is a good start to finding a new and better way.

Father, I am so tired of myself!
It seems that I can't do anything right.
Because I feel miserable and worried that I'm failing,
I'm difficult to be around.
I'm ignoring the comfort and wisdom of those who care for
me, or even driving them away.
Lord, I don't know what's going on with me!
But I know it's not what I want.
Help me to find my way back to You and to my life, my
friends, my family.
Disperse the cloud that seems to envelop me, Father.
Remind me that I am Your child, Your creation.
When my lips form around a mean word, let me instead
breathe Your name.
When my insecurity nudges me to put down another,
let me remember that, as Your son, Jesus lifted up everyone.
When my behavior becomes mired in negativity,
give me the clarity to recognize and change it.
Most of all, Lord, give me the courage to examine myself, my
thoughts, my life honestly.
When I shrink from admitting my own responsibility,
make me brave enough to acknowledge my weaknesses
and mistakes.
When I feel that big changes are too hard,
give me the strength to make at least one small change.
Let me listen to Your still, small voice in my ear,
Let me respond to Your gentle tap on my shoulder.

Prayer for Self-Forgiveness

Whether you have experienced a serious failure or a small one, whether you have blamed yourself or denied your responsibility, whether you have hurt yourself or those who love you, forgiveness is the most powerful healing agent you can seek. God is always ready to forgive. We, on the other hand, are not always ready to bring our failings to Him, or to forgive ourselves. You can begin the process by asking forgiveness of God, from others whom you may have hurt and for help in forgiving yourself. A prayer like this one may help you get started:

Father, You know my weaknesses, my disabilities, my failings,
and now, as always, You offer me a choice:
I can continue in my misery, or I can confess my failings
and ask You to forgive me.
O Lord, I do confess my failings and I do ask You
with all my heart to forgive me.
I know that You hear me and that You forgive me, Lord,
yesterday, today, tomorrow.
I trust in You, Lord, more than I trust in myself.
I thank You for allowing me to reach this point, the point
where I must turn to You and seek Your mercy, Your help.
Lord, though I'm sure of You, I'm not always so sure of myself.
Help me to honestly evaluate my life, my strengths
and my weaknesses.

When I have looked inside, let me then turn outside;
Open my heart so that I can ask forgiveness of those I've hurt.
Even if they are not prepared to forgive me, prepare me,
Lord, to ask.
Then give me the strength to truly forgive myself
for my mistakes and my failings.
In seeking forgiveness of You, of others, of myself,
I am choosing a new life, Lord.
Give me strength for this new journey.

GOD'S NEW START

There are times when focusing on your failures can be an exercise in futility, and one that can keep you from appreciating God's guiding hand in your life.

A while ago, I was telling my friend Marilyn about my unfortunate habit of panicking when I'm late and find myself behind a particularly slow driver, in a long line or stuck talking to someone I hadn't expected to see. All I can think of is that not only am I late, but that the slow driver, long line or unplanned conversation is making me even later! I end up frustrated with myself and angry with anything or anyone that gets in my way.

Marilyn had an interesting perspective. "I know just what you mean. I used to find myself with a bad case of road rage when I was late," said my soft-spoken friend. "I'd pound on the steering wheel and yell at people who couldn't possibly hear me. But then one afternoon when I was late and fuming, the traffic came to a standstill. By the time I'd inched up enough to see what was going on, I realized it was more than the usual rush-hour clogging. There'd been a two-car accident. By the time I came up to the place where it had happened, the ambulance was pulling away and the trucks had come to take away the mangled cars. All I could think was that if I had left any earlier—if I'd been on time—I might have been right there when the accident occurred. I could have been part of it or even have made it worse!

"I said a prayer for the victims, and I also thanked God that I was late that day. And it made me think that maybe some of my weaknesses or bad habits aren't so much real failures but just opportunities for God to put me on another, maybe safer, path."

Marilyn helped me see that not every failure or weakness is something I can explain, or even understand. And maybe I shouldn't try so hard to comprehend every seemingly negative situation. Yes, I can and should recognize bad patterns and the need to change them, but I needn't search out the origin of every difficulty in my life. Rather than desperately seeking the "why and how" for each perceived failure, I should focus on where God wants to lead me now. Only God can utterly transform failure into success.

Even if we give up on ourselves, it always turns out that God has other plans. As my prayer partner often proclaims, "All to the glory and praise of God." When Jesus is about to show the glory of God by performing a miracle, He tells His disciples that the blind man they see

> ". . . *was born blind so that God's works might be revealed in him. We must work the works of him who sent me while it is day; night is coming when no one can work. As long as I am in the world, I am the light of the world.*" —JOHN 9:3–5

And so, when you are stymied in your prayers by failures and shortcomings, you might pray by crying aloud with all your heart and mind the words of those perceived failures whom God made successful through their encounter with Jesus. As you repeat the words of the faithful men and women who struggled with failure, you'll begin to understand how similar your experiences are to theirs.

- Pray with the leper who falls to his knees when he sees Jesus and says, "Lord, if You choose, You can make me clean" (Matthew 8:2).

- Pray with the hemorrhaging woman who creeps up behind Jesus and touches the fringe of His cloak, saying, "If I only touch His cloak, I will be made well" (Matthew 9:21).

- Pray with the Canaanite woman whose daughter was said to be possessed, who kneels before Jesus and says, "Lord, help me." When Jesus seems to reject her plea, she insists, "Lord . . . even the dogs eat the crumbs that fall from their masters' table" (Matthew 15:25, 27).

- Pray with the crowd that witnessed Jesus healing, "He has done everything well; he even makes the deaf to hear and the mute to speak" (Mark 7:37).

- Pray with the blind Bartimaeus, who, when Jesus is about to pass him by, shouts, "Jesus, Son of David, have mercy on me!" And when those around him try to silence him, "he cried out even more loudly, 'Son of David, have mercy on me!'" When Jesus finally asks what he wants, Bartimaeus confidently responds, "My teacher, let me see again" (Mark 10:47, 48, 51).

- Pray with the centurion asking Jesus to heal his servant, "Lord, do not trouble yourself, for I am not worthy to have you come under my roof . . . . But only speak the word, and let my servant be healed" (Luke 7:6–8).

- Pray with Zacchaeus the hated tax collector, converted and willing to admit his sins, who says to the Lord, "Look, half of my possessions, Lord, I will give to the poor; and if I have defrauded anyone of anything, I will pay back four times as much" (Luke 19:8).

- Pray with the Samaritan woman, who, when Jesus tells her about living water, says, "Sir, give me this water, so that I may never be thirsty" (John 4:15).

- Pray with Peter still carrying the weight of his failure, who answers Jesus, "Yes, Lord; you know that I love you."

Jesus asks him again. Peter answers again, "Yes, Lord; you know that I love you." Jesus asks him yet again, and Peter, who denied the Lord three times, wipes away his failure when he answers the third time, "Lord, you know everything; you know that I love you" (John 21:15–17).

It is important to observe that all these failures that were made into the Lord's successes shared one trait: a willingness to seek out Jesus and follow His instructions. Rather than allowing bitterness to overwhelm them, they yearned for the Lord. They did not deny their own weaknesses and failings; they did not simply admit these problems and sit around feeling sorry for themselves; they did not blame others; they did not blame themselves; and they did not accuse God of rejecting them. They acknowledged their problems and actively turned to the Lord for help, and even when that help did not appear to be instantly forthcoming—as with the Canaanite woman who courageously endured humiliation at the initial dismissal of Jesus—they persisted in seeking out the Lord. They persisted in *prayer*. And when their failures were wiped away and healed; when God gave them a brand-new start, they gave thanks. And then they proceeded to live it.

THANKSGIVING

Feelings of failure often get in the way of feelings of thanks. When you feel that you've failed, you may not see anything about yourself or your life to be thankful for. These suggested

prayers of gratitude are meant to encourage you to acknowledge the presence of God in your heart and in the world
around you.

> *Creator of all, thank You for giving me life out of Your*
> *perfection and love.*

> *Jesus, thank You for showing me in Your love for all*
> *those who came to You that You are able and willing to*
> *welcome and redeem me.*

> *Lord, thank You for the people in my life who believe in*
> *me even when I cannot believe in myself.*

> *Dear God, thank You for the opportunity to learn from*
> *my mistakes and grow closer to You.*

> *Father, thank You for the many daily reminders I have*
> *that no one but You is perfect, and therefore, that I am*
> *certainly not alone.*

PSALM-AS-PRAYER

This psalm is particularly helpful for those of us who feel
that we've failed because it focuses on God's power to transform. The psalm is the cry of one who feels weak and abandoned, and yet knows that God, in His great and abiding
power, will offer salvation and hope.

PSALM 77:2–15
GOD'S MIGHTY DEEDS RECALLED

I cry aloud to God,
aloud to God, that he may hear me.
In the day of my trouble I seek the Lord;
in the night my hand is stretched out without wearying;
my soul refuses to be comforted.
I think of God, and I moan;
I meditate, and my spirit faints.
You keep my eyelids from closing;
I am so troubled that I cannot speak.
I consider the days of old,
and remember the years of long ago.
I commune with my heart in the night;
I meditate and search my spirit;
"Will the Lord spurn forever,
and never again be favorable?
Has his steadfast love ceased for ever?
Are his promises at an end for all time?
Has God forgotten to be gracious?
Has he in anger shut up his compassion?
And I say, "It is my grief that the right hand
of the Most High has changed."
I will call to mind the deeds of the Lord;
I will remember your wonders of old.
I will meditate on all your work,
and muse on your mighty deeds.

Your way, O God, is holy.
What god is so great as our God?
You are the God who works wonders.
You have displayed your might among the peoples.
With your strong arm you redeemed your people,
the descendants of Jacob and Joseph.

Suggested Closing Prayer

Father, I feel lost. I feel as if everything I touch withers. I've made mistakes; I've taken serious missteps. If I can't find my way in my world, how can I ever find my way to You? Why, really, would You bother with me? And yet, somewhere deep inside, I know that You not only bother with me, but that You love me! Let me take courage from that knowledge and seek Your love and guidance. The things of this world are not as important as Your love. Although I may have failed, I ask You to forgive my despair and keep me close to You. Let me learn from my mistakes, and keep my face turned to the light that is Your presence.

Bible Reference

At that moment, the cock crowed for the second time. Then Peter remembered that Jesus had said to him, "Before the cock crows twice, you will deny me three times." And he broke down and wept. —MARK 14:72

When You Need to Trust

AS WE'VE SEEN throughout this book, there are times when it's hard to take even a single step along the way of prayer. At other times, we feel we could scale a mountain without breathing hard just to get closer to God. For most of us, the prayer journey to trust in God takes a lifetime. Yet by deciding to patiently and faithfully undertake this journey, knowing that a deeper relationship with God is both our objective and our reward, we can get a glimpse of that joy along the way, long before we arrive at our destination.

But what does it really mean to say that the successful prayer journey leads to God? How will we know if we've reached God? How can we tell if we're actually close to God, the goal of our journey, or whether we are just experiencing the exuberance of a "second wind" in prayer?

Whether you are currently reclining at a rest stop, scurrying up the mountain or slipping in the mud, the summit of prayer remains the same: a relationship with God so complete that anxiety, fear and anger melt away. It's the kind of trust that says, "Whatever happens to me, Lord, I trust in You. I do not fear failure, poverty, abandonment, illness or death, because I know that You are with me."

While you may get a glimpse of this kind of trust, not many of us have reached this place in our relationship with God. Still, you can take comfort in knowing that God is with you even as you seek Him. Often the best you can do is to simply stay on the path, even if you've come to a temporary stop, even if you feel you're moving backward. Your steps may falter, but you needn't worry. God understands all this. Most of us are not saints yet!

WAITING ON THE LORD

God is always with us, but in our busyness, we don't often allow ourselves to experience His presence. One way—a challenging but very rewarding way—to become more aware of God's presence in our lives is to wait on the Lord. By just being still and focusing your thoughts on God, you can make a space for contemplation in the midst of your obligations and duties.

Martha and Mary provide the perfect examples of how we're often unaware of the presence of the Lord and how to wait for Him. When Jesus visited the sisters at their Bethany home, Martha began to try to get everything ready to provide hospitality to Jesus. She had wonderful intentions—she was ready to "wait on the Lord" in the sense of serving Him. Luke tells us that Martha

> . . . had a sister named Mary, who sat at the Lord's feet
> and listened to what he was saying. But Martha was

distracted by her many tasks; so she came to him and asked, "Lord, do you not care that my sister has left me to do all the work by myself? Tell her then to help me." But the Lord answered her, "Martha, Martha, you are worried and distracted by many things; there is need of only one thing. Mary has chosen the better part, which will not be taken away from her." —LUKE 10:39–42

Poor Martha! Was she wrong to try to serve Jesus? Of course not. But Martha was so intent on serving the man that she failed to recognize the Messiah.

SITTING QUIETLY IN THE PRESENCE OF THE LORD

On one day each week, I say no verbal prayers except for the prayers my husband and I start and end our day with. Recognizing my tendency to be like Martha—busy and distracted—I use my once-a-week silence to be quiet in the presence of the Lord. For me, that silence requires trust. Like Martha, I'm not one to wait—my prayers are often a barrage of pleas and praise—and so by making myself wait on the Lord in stillness, I'm expressing my faith in the most challenging way I can: in silence and patience. My day of silence, my prayer Sabbath, restores my sense of unity with the Lord.

The day before my day of silent prayer, I pray like this:

Dear Lord,

Tomorrow let me pray to You without words and images.

Let my prayer to You be the living of my life in the knowledge and awareness of Your constant presence, love, forgiveness, mercy, healing.

And by so living, let my life itself become a prayer to You, without the need for words or images.

If you'd like to prepare for a weekly prayer Sabbath, take comfort from Jesus' assurances about waiting on and trusting the Lord. I've found that these words of the Lord are helpful miniprayers before a period of silence.

When I find myself asking the Lord for healing as I would a human doctor who needs constant reminders of what I need, I'm strengthened by Jesus' instruction,

> *"When you are praying, do not heap up empty phrases as the Gentiles do; for they think that they will be heard because of their many words. Do not be like them, for your Father knows what you need before you ask him."*
>
> —MATTHEW 6:7–8

When I feel guilty for my failings, and I've been praying repeatedly for forgiveness, I turn to Jesus' call to Levi to be an apostle:

> *And as he sat at dinner in Levi's house, many tax collectors and sinners were also sitting with Jesus and his*

disciples—for there were many who followed him. When the scribes of the Pharisees saw that he was eating with sinners and tax collectors, they said to his disciples, "Why does he eat with tax collectors and sinners?" When Jesus heard this, he said to them, "Those who are well have no need of a physician, but those who are sick; I have come to call not the righteous but sinners."   —MARK 2:15–17

If I'm worried about a project I'm working on and repeatedly ask God for success, I read Jesus' counsel on worrying about worldly things:

Therefore do not worry, saying, "What will we eat?" or "What will we drink?" or "What will we wear?" For it is the Gentiles who strive for all these things; and indeed your heavenly Father knows that you need all these things. But strive first for the kingdom of God and his righteousness, and all these things will be given to you as well.   —MATTHEW 6:31–33

When I feel compelled to offer the Lord professions of my love as if He needed constant reassurance of my attention and devotion, I can turn to the testament of the One Who was One with Jesus,

Now when all the people were baptized, and when Jesus also had been baptized and was praying, the heaven was opened, and the Holy Spirit descended upon him

in bodily form like a dove. And a voice came from heaven, "You are my Son, the Beloved; with you I am well pleased."   —LUKE 3:21–22

When I am weak and begging God to increase my faith, I straighten myself out by reading about the father of the sick son who begged Jesus:

"If you are able to do anything, have pity on us and help us." Jesus said to him, "If you are able!—All things can be done for the one who believes." Immediately the father of the child cried out, "I believe; help my unbelief!"   —MARK 9:22–24

A prayer Sabbath or break requires both the training of prayer and the silence of trust. Like an athlete who takes off one day a week from training in order to settle her mind and allow her body to recover, I emerge from my quiet day with a stronger sense of God's constant presence in my life.

"I Will Give You Rest"

During a prayer Sabbath, you may want to concentrate on Jesus' invitation to rest in Him, an invitation that contains the key to the trust that empowers both spoken prayer and silent devotion:

"Come to me, all you that are weary and are carrying heavy burdens, and I will give you rest. Take my yoke

upon you, and learn from me, for I am gentle and humble in heart, and you will find rest for your souls. For my yoke is easy, and my burden is light.

—MATTHEW 11:28–30

When I'm stuck on the path to God, stuck in my prayer, I take great comfort in these verses. The truth is, I need a time of rest to know how far I've come (or how far back I've slipped!) and where I hope to go. So much of everyone's prayer life is spent waiting, resting, in the Lord. After all, no matter what we might think, He's the One doing the heavy lifting in our relationship.

As I rest and wait, I have a choice to make. I can let my mind fill up with fear, anger, doubt and self-pity; or I can rest and wait in a state of trust, knowing that Jesus invited and instructed me to do just that. I know this isn't as easy as it sounds. There are times when I'm so paralyzed by fear that I can hardly breathe, never mind wait trustfully for God. We all have such times, and again, God understands. He is infinitely more patient than He asks us to be.

On the other hand, we're not helpless or unable to make an effort in seeking to wait on the Lord. We're not the pitiful victims of our errant feelings. God stands ready to help us always. He has made the offer: *Rest in Me. Wait on Me.* Knowing this, with His always-present help, we can imagine a safe and peaceful rest. We can deliberately put a space between our negative feelings and ourselves as we rest. You may already be doing this through some relaxation techniques, but you can also try these exercises to help you rest in prayer.

Go to a room where you feel comfortable and sit or lie down in a relaxing position. Try to calm your mind. Picture a chair or a table across the room. If there isn't one where you are, imagine one. Imagine that there is nothing else in the room but you and the empty surface of that table or chair. Now gather all your "obstacle" feelings—the worry, fear, anger, doubt or sadness that may be keeping you from resting in the Lord—into one mass of string. The different feelings may have different colors and even textures. Allow the feelings/strings to become intermingled with one another, knotted together, completely tangled. Study the messy mass of string in front of you.

Now imagine that you're sending the tangled mass of string over to the surface of the table or chair. Let it go. You're putting it away for now. Once it has settled onto the empty surface, imagine there's a wall with a door between you and the feelings/strings. The door is closed. Those feelings have left you so that you can seek the peace, the rest that Jesus invites you to. Close your eyes and repeat His promise, "I will give you rest." Continue to repeat this softly, allowing your body and mind to relax. Allow yourself to be cradled in His peace. Confident in His promise and presence, rest from your burdens for a time.

When you are ready, imagine that you are rising gently

and approaching the door. Know that Jesus will remain with you as you move forward into your day. Open the door. Look at the surface of the table or chair. You may be surprised now, because when you look down at your tangled mass of feelings/strings, all the strings are separated. They are lying next to one another in straight, untangled, unknotted lines. You can identify each feeling and view it calmly. Decide which—if any—you want to carry out with you. Remember that you can leave them where they are. However, if you do choose to carry them with you, remember that Jesus' invitation remains yours: "I will give you rest." You can lay down those feelings again at any time.

LIVING PRAYER

The last time I visited my good friend Gwen in Key West, she told me, "I've been pursuing peace for a long time. What I've finally realized is that peace isn't something to pursue, it's something to grow inside myself. Now I don't have to stop whatever I'm doing to pray. I feel that every moment of my life is a prayer."

As Gwen continued to talk, I realized that "living prayer" was more a way of life than a formal prayer. And I understood that living prayer was the next step toward complete trust.

In saying that her life was a prayer, Gwen meant that

everything she did, every thought she had, every word she spoke, grew out of her sense that God was with her. Gwen's living prayer was the result of many years of praying and searching. Those of us who haven't yet experienced that level of prayer can at least dedicate a particular period of time to try living prayer.

The process may feel a little uncomfortable at first, but it can teach you a new way to be close to God, even if you're not able to continue it indefinitely. However, if you do commit yourself to this kind of prayer, you may find it becoming more natural and easy every day.

It's important to know that living prayer won't be the answer to all your problems. Gwen's life isn't perfect. Like everyone else, those who practice living prayer sometimes feel down, discouraged and as if they've failed. But living prayer isn't about living in a dream world where everything is exactly right. Living prayer is about living always in the presence of God.

A day of living prayer, whether expressed in words or thoughts or both, might go something like this:

- Wake up and thank God for your day, for your life. Ask for help as you face the day's challenges.

- Thank God that you are able to get up and start the day. Ask His help in dealing with your aches, pains and other health problems.

- When you shower or bathe, thank God for the miracle of the water, the fresh-smelling soap, the minty toothpaste, the scented shampoo.

- As you eat your breakfast, savor the taste even if you're in a hurry, thanking God for food and drink. Pray for those who are hungry, and ask God to help you to help meet the needs of all of His children.

- As you begin your daily work, whether it's at home or elsewhere, manual or mental, thank God for your colleagues and family members, even those who irritate or frustrate you. If you work alone, give thanks for the peace of solitude. Offer your labor to God, asking Him to help you to perform it well. Pray particularly for anyone you will meet today who is likely to be difficult and for the grace to handle the situation.

- As you interact with the people around you, pray for them and pray that you will be a good influence in their lives. Offer special thanks for those who have a positive influence on you.

- As you notice the weather, thank God for the miracle of nature, for good weather and for shelter in bad weather. Pray for those who must travel in dangerous weather.

- When you read or hear the news of the day, thank God for the peace and stability in your life. Pray for those who

have no peace, and that world and local leaders will be
guided by the Lord.

↜ When you break for lunch, gratefully taste whatever food
and drink you have, thanking God for the chance to rest.
Praise Him for the flowers, the trees, the snowflakes or
whatever of His good creation you encounter.

↜ If you have time for exercise during the day, ask God for
a healing, healthy workout and thank Him for your body.

↜ When you return to work, recommit yourself and thank
God again for the opportunity and ability to work.

↜ When you're returning home from work, offer thanks for
your transportation whether it's a car, bike, train, subway
or your own feet. Pray for the safety of all who are traveling.

↜ Begin your evening by praising God for time to eat, rest
or complete any of the day's unfinished work. Give
thanks for those you're enjoying your evening with. If
you're alone, remember that God is with you and thank
Him for His presence. Pray for the people you know who
are troubled and for patience with them.

↜ At dinner, enjoy your meal slowly, praising God again for
His provision. As you finish your chores, thank Him for
the chance to get them done and for rest from labor.

- ☙ If you read before going to bed, thank God for eyes to see and a mind to discern. If you watch television or a movie, thank God for the time and technology that allows you to enjoy them.

- ☙ As you get ready for bed, again be grateful for hot water and soft towels.

- ☙ As you lie down to sleep, thank God for the day. Ask for forgiveness for your failures and mistakes, thank Him for your successes and ask Him for healing rest.

Occasionally God blesses those of us who are on the path but have not yet arrived at the place of trust with a glimpse of what it is like to live prayer, to live in Him. If we are ready for these glimmers, if we can accept them, they can prove to be breathtaking catalysts for our journey.

～

Earlier this year, my eye doctor told me he'd found the beginnings of cataracts in both of my eyes. I couldn't believe it! At thirty-six, I got a diagnosis of cancer and now at forty-four, I had signs of cataracts—not to mention a number of other dismaying problems in between. Granted, the doctor was full of assurances—"No real trouble for some time . . . highly treatable." Why me? What next? A hearing aid?

To make matters worse, my mother had just had cataract operations on both eyes, and they had not gone well.

Apparently she is one of the few who did not take well to the surgery. Would the same thing happen to me three decades later? Was it genetic? And just where did I get these genes anyway? Was it too late to trade them in?

When I finally finished my extended pity party, I settled down to do some imaging prayer. As I've said, I'd done this for years, especially after the melanoma diagnosis. I would imagine God healing the places that were hurt or diseased, or that might become hurt or diseased. I believed in this type of prayer and I found it soothing. I felt God's presence when I did imaging prayer. And although I'd stopped stewing about my ridiculous body and all its problems, I was badly in need of soothing.

I went to a quiet place where I could hear the waves of the river gently lapping outside our door and the boats bumping against their docks. I sat comfortably on the couch and relaxed. I breathed deeply. I already knew what I would envision: Jesus holding me close, my head leaning upon His shoulder. After a few moments like this, I moved to the next part of the prayer. I planned to imagine Jesus moving His hand softly over my eyes and closing them as He held His hand there, healing them.

But that's not what happened. When I tried to move to the next part of the prayer, I didn't imagine Jesus moving His hand. Instead, He kept it on my head, still holding me close. I was confused. What was happening? Why weren't things going as I'd planned? Suddenly, I felt God's calming presence fill me, and I sensed Him saying: *I have given you eyes for you to use. Use them now. Use them always. See everything. Notice everything. Hold what you see in your heart. It will always be there. Your husband's beautiful, smiling blue eyes. The river rushing outside your door after the ferry has passed by. The full moon rising in the sky. The eastern star. Your family on Christmas day. Books. Flowers. Hummingbirds. See it all. Know it is from Me. Remember. And leave the rest to Me.*

And I know that for that brief time, I experienced living prayer. The prayer I had in mind meant nothing, and for once I didn't care. That's a place I want to visit as often as I can; I want to live there.

Hand in Hand with God

God has blessed me in my friends, some of whom are much farther along in their prayer journeys than I am. I do my best to learn from them. My friend Marcia has honored me by sharing her extraordinary life and faith. The more I've learned about her, the more I've come to understand what it means to live in absolute trust.

Marcia hasn't lived a quiet, retired or sheltered life. Quite the opposite. In 1948, when she was just twenty, she left her family in Johannesburg, South Africa, to go to Israel and help defend the refugees who flooded into the country after World War II. After some training and a long, dangerous trip north to Rome and then southeast to Israel, Marcia found herself serving as a meteorologist in the Israeli Air Force. After being demobilized in 1949, she remained in Israel for more than a year. Then, on a visit to her family in South Africa, she met and married a local farmer.

She and her husband lived in Johannesburg, raising two sons and two daughters as they became successful farmers. After her husband died, Marcia knew it was time to leave the farm and the increasingly dangerous land of South Africa behind. She sold the farming business and then helped her adult children and their families leave the country where she'd spent most of her life. "I wanted each of them to have their own lives," she recalls with no regret in her voice. "I didn't want them to feel tied to the business or the country when they had their whole lives in front of them."

Today, all of Marcia's children and grandchildren are successful, and she lives near three of her children and their families in Connecticut while frequently visiting her fourth daughter's family in Australia. She has visited Israel, China, England and many other countries that most of us can hardly find on a map. The terrorism since 2001 hasn't slowed her down. Now in her late seventies, she never hesitates to embrace a new adventure, whether it's writing a memoir or traveling to Australia for a family birthday party. When I asked her if she was ever afraid or if the trips ever seemed too daunting, she said, "You know, I believe that when you go out the door, God takes your hand."

I think about Marcia's words often, and when I do, I

remember the old gospel song that begins, "Put your hand in the hand of the Man who stilled the waters. Put your hand in the hand of the Man who calmed the sea." As a child, I loved that song! It seemed to fit so easily in my ears, mind and heart. I remember so clearly how it comforted me when I was too young to know what my life would become. The words to that song, like Marcia's declaration, said everything there was to say about faith: Put your hand in God's hand and all will be as it should. And that is trust.

Now, after a life of prayer and seeking God, after crushing failures and astonishing successes, after times of perfect health and times of terrifying illness, I think about Jesus' admonition to the disciples who tried to keep Him from the village children:

> *"Let the little children come to me, and do not stop them; for it is to such as these that the kingdom of heaven belongs."*   —MATTHEW 19:14

Can we do as innocent, wholly trusting children would, and put our hands in the hand of the Man who stilled the waters?

THANKSGIVING

The state of complete trust is the state of continual thanksgiving. As you work to grow in trust, giving thanks often and sincerely can help you along on the journey and remind you of your objective: communion with God. As you seek God, praise Him continually for every good thing in life.

Lord, thank You for my body in all its amazing and miraculous workings.

God, thank You for my will and my spirit, and turn them increasingly toward You.

Father, thank You for the voice with which I can and must praise You.

Jesus, thank You for providing me with Your perfect example.

Lord, thank You for the creation that manifests Your love and constant attention.

Psalm-as-Prayer

PSALM 117: UNIVERSAL CALL TO WORSHIP

Praise the Lord, all you nations!
Extol him, all you peoples!
For great is his steadfast love toward us,
and the faithfulness of the Lord endures forever.
Praise the Lord!

Suggested Closing Prayer

Father, I've heard about people who have faith so great that everything they say and do is an act of prayer. I don't know if I have the capacity for such faith, for such prayer; I hope I do. O Lord, I yearn to grow in trust. Guide me, Lord. Teach me to wait on You and to take my rest as You offer it on this journey. Help me to keep my focus on You so that I cannot help but move forward.

Bible Reference

While Jesus was standing there, he cried out, "Let anyone who is thirsty come to me, and let the one who believes in me drink. As the scripture has said, 'Out of the believer's heart shall flow rivers of living water.'" Now he said this about the Spirit, which believers in him were to receive. . . .   —JOHN 7:37–39